I0819459

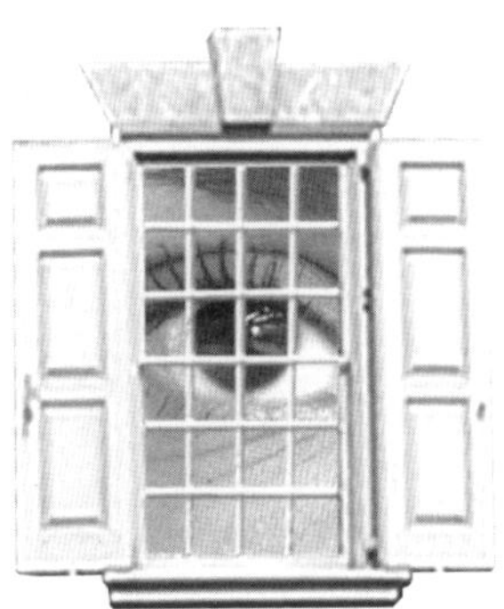

# DECLARATION HOUSE

# DECLARATION HOUSE

Edited by

Anna Arabindan-Kesson, Paul M. Farber,

and Yolanda Wisher

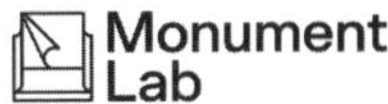


TEMPLE UNIVERSITY PRESS 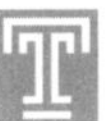 *Philadelphia Rome Tokyo*

TEMPLE UNIVERSITY PRESS
Philadelphia, Pennsylvania 19122
*tupress.temple.edu*


Published 2026

Library of Congress Cataloging-in-Publication Data

Names: Arabindan-Kesson, Anna, editor, contributor. | Farber, Paul M., 1982– editor, contributor. | Wisher, Yolanda, editor, contributor. | Monument Lab (Art studio), producer of exhibition.
Title: Declaration House / edited by Anna Arabindan-Kesson, Paul M. Farber, and Yolanda Wisher.
Description: Philadelphia : Temple University Press, 2026. | The public artwork "The Descendants of Monticello," curated by Monument Lab, was installed at Declaration House in Philadelphia from June 24–December 1, 2024. | Includes bibliographical references and index. | Summary: "Essays, poems, conversations, and artworks related to the art installation The Descendants of Monticello and the Declaration House site in Philadelphia"— Provided by publisher.
Identifiers: LCCN 2026008985 (print) | LCCN 2026008986 (ebook) | ISBN 9781439927649 (paperback) | ISBN 9781439927656 (pdf)
Subjects: LCSH: Clark, Sonya. Descendants of Monticello. | Hemmings, Robert, 1762–1819. | United States. Declaration of Independence. | Declaration House (Philadelphia, Pa.) | Hemings family. | Public art—Pennsylvania—Philadelphia. | Video installations (Art)—Pennsylvania—Philadelphia. | BISAC: HISTORY / United States / State & Local / Middle Atlantic (DC, DE, MD, NJ, NY, PA) | SOCIAL SCIENCE / Slavery
Classification: LCC N6537.C4987 (print) | LCC N6537.C4987 (ebook)
LC record available at https://lccn.loc.gov/2026008985
LC ebook record available at https://lccn.loc.gov/2026008986

The manufacturer's authorized representative in the EU for product safety is Temple University Rome, Via di San Sebastianello, 16, 00187 Rome RM, Italy (https://rome.temple.edu/). tempress@temple.edu

♾ The paper used in this publication meets the requirements of the American National Standard for Information Sciences—Permanence of Paper for Printed Library Materials, ANSI Z39.48–1992

Printed in the United States of America

9 8 7 6 5 4 3 2 1

*For Robert Hemmings and*

*all the Descendants of Monticello*

I have said that the Declaration of Independence is the ring-bolt to the chain of your nation's destiny; so, indeed, I regard it. The principles contained in that instrument are saving principles. Stand by those principles, be true to them on all occasions, in all places, against all foes, and at whatever cost.

—Frederick Douglass,
"What to the Slave Is the Fourth of July?," July 5, 1852

---

All eyes are opened, or opening, to the rights of man.

—Thomas Jefferson,
Letter to Roger Weightman, June 24, 1826

# Contents

# Watchword: Seers

Jane Kamensky

If you had the good fortune to round the corner of Seventh and Market Streets in Philadelphia during the back half of 2024, you found yourself confronted with an experience of the uncanny as a set of eyes, each taller than an adult human, peered at you from the windows of the National Park Service's Declaration House.

The building itself is crumbling, derelict: a forgotten pseudo-monument dating to the U.S. bicentennial in 1976 and pretending to be something much older. But oh, those eyes—crinkling, twinkling, sometimes even winking. Witnessing, sure, but that sounds too passive. The watchers in the windows take your measure, eye-to-eye. *Their* windows peer into *our* souls. Long relegated to the margins of citizenship for generations, as Robert Hemmings was consigned to Thomas Jefferson's garret, Sonya Clark insists that the eyes have it: run of the house, outside-in. What do they make of the passersby? They *are* us; we are they; together, We the People.

This is Clark's installation "The Descendants of Monticello," which makes its profound intervention in art and in history by flipping the gaze. As an enslaved valet, Robert Hemmings may well have stood at Jefferson's elbow as the Virginia congressman drafted the immortal, aspirational words *all men are created equal*. The framers at the nearby Pennsylvania State House would have seen Hemmings regularly. Yet his position meant for him to be looked past, overlooked. Certainly he was never portrayed, never *centered*. Clark's window lights frame him in the grand manner. Her conjuring transforms the unseen witness into the seer.

To meet the gaze is to stand equal: *I see you, know you,* am *you*. To perform their subjection, enslaved people were expected, by those who bought and owned and sold them, to look away. When they stole themselves, writing with their bodies the most visceral examples of declaring independence and pursuing happiness, their would-be captors often described their "down look." By one historian's count, the down look constituted "the single most frequent label for fugitives' appearance," a common trope across the tens of thousands of runaway ads whose placement fees kept newspapers afloat from Charleston to Boston.[1]

"The Descendants of Monticello" would roll their animated eyes at the very notion of the down look. They peer out, over, at, through—down-lookers become God's eyes. They have earned fury, and their gaze might well be righteous: *It was you!* But the genius of Clark's work—and of the descendants' engagement with her camera, and with their viewers—is much subtler. The eyes upon us seem neither angry nor mournful. They dance, they play, brimming with a powerful sense of inner life—of personhood—that the system of chattel slavery strove always to deny. The eyes appear, in many cases, playful, even joyful. An eyebrow lifts, a smize unfurls. Are they sharing a joke? Are we in on it, its target, or maybe both?

As Clark's "The Descendants of Monticello" inverts the gaze, it blurs time. The giant eyes in ye olde windows belong to both the quick and the dead. Clark reanimates historical daguerreotypes and old family photographs, placing ancestral eyes side by side with those of people making change in the here and now. Even upon close examination, even for somebody who has the privilege of working with some of the living Hemmings descendants, it is very difficult to distinguish ancestors from the living, past from present.

Our democracy requires that very blurring: a commitment to a shared future that rests upon unflinching knowledge of a still-living past. To see and be seen by Robert Hemmings is to pluralize our origin stories: to recognize that *founders* encompassed the multitude of Americans—Black and white and brown and red, young and old, female and male—who imagined a land of liberty. To take stock of the teenager who filled the inkwell alongside the man who held the quill. To *hold these truths,* Clark challenges us, requires new ways of seeing and being seen. The poems, essays, artworks, and conversations gathered in this volume take up that challenge, pushing us in new directions. Sometimes they disagree with each other, and sometimes I disagree with them. That's precisely as it should be.

Clark's work also invites, even demands, democratic action. To acknowledge Robert Hemmings and his kinfolk as founders means to realize what self-government demands of each of us. We, too, are re-founders of our constitutional democracy, every day. Are we up to the task? Can we stare back at those windows along Market Street with an equal sense of self-possession? The watchers remind us: One day, history will see us plain. Let us make ourselves worthy of its gaze.

## NOTE

1. Jonathan Prude, "To Look upon the 'Lower Sort': Runaway Ads and the Appearance of Unfree Laborers in America, 1750–1800," *Journal of American History* 78, no. 1 (1991): 124–159, https://doi.org/10.2307/2078091.

# Preface

Anna Arabindan-Kesson, Paul M. Farber,

and Yolanda Wisher

This is a book about a house, in a city of row houses, at the faultline of democracy and belonging. A house in Old City Philadelphia that is remarkable and mundane, ordinary and uncanny. A symbol of birth and demolition. A site of freedom and enslavement. An artifact of authorship and erasure. Its dualities are overwhelming and grounding.

This book is also about the founding of the nation. It is about the radical potential and glaring inconsistencies of its originating document, the Declaration of Independence, as well as the protagonists of that moment, and the generations that carry its promise forward. A nation, to this day, still young in its fragile democracy and entrenched in its troubled histories. Traumatized, but also transformed by those who find pathways to healing, learning, and belonging.

The Declaration House, as we now understand it, sits on the historic location where Thomas Jefferson and Robert Hemmings spent several months in Philadelphia during the drafting of the Declaration of Independence in 1776. Jefferson, then thirty-three years old, was in Philadelphia, representing Virginia at the Second Continental Congress, where he served as principal author of the declaration. Hemmings, then fourteen years old, was the half brother of Jefferson's wife, Martha Wayles Skelton. Hemmings was an enslaved valet brought to Philadelphia by Jefferson from his Monticello plantation in Charlottesville, Virginia. From May to September 1776, Jefferson lived in a rented house at Seventh and Market Streets. There, early in the summer, he worked on the Declaration of Independence until it was approved by Congress. Delegates to the Second Continental Congress adopted the document on July 4 and signed it on August 2 at the nearby Pennsylvania State House (now Independence Hall). For the duration of their stay in Philadelphia, Hemmings attended to Jefferson, including taking care of his clothing, food, and personal matters. He likely slept in a hallway or attic on the upper level of the house.

The original Declaration House residence in which Jefferson and Hemmings stayed was owned by Jacob and Maria Graff, who operated brickyards in the city. Ownership of the house changed hands until 1883, when the structure was torn down. Other buildings that stood on this site included a bank designed by noted Philadelphia architect Frank Furness and a hot-dog stand named Tom Thumb. In 1975, in preparation for America's bicentennial, the National Park Service's Independence National Historical Park built a replica of the Graff House with an additional wing for exhibits and incorporated several fragments of the original house into its facade. While originally open to the public, in recent years the house has been closed in advance of renovations and efforts to increase accessibility.

The U.S. Declaration of Independence, drafted at this site, began the path toward freedom from British rule in thirteen American colonies and went on to have a profound and lasting influence on world history. The opening lines of the declaration—including the words "we hold these truths to be self-evident, that all men are created equal"—are so well known that it can be easy to forget how transformative they were as a statement of freedom. Since its writing, this document has inspired approximately 120 other "declarations of independence" by nations and peoples around the world. And yet these words were authored by a man who held others in bondage, even as he knew that slavery was a profound moral wrong.[1]

The Declaration House holds the weight of our history, but as is often the case with historical sites and monuments, it obscures our understanding of a fuller narrative of the nation. The house stood on the outskirts of a colonial city that was lived in for more than ten thousand years by the Lenape peoples before it was founded. The name "Declaration House" was not part of its original imprint—it was a rental property, a colonial "Airbnb"—but its reemergence over the course of a century's time following its demolition consolidates the history of the nation's founding site into two words and one author of American democracy. Its most famous resident lived there only briefly, as a renter. The house stood on the edges of the city, and as the development of the colonial city moved west, it fell prey to its own form of gentrification. However, if we approach this site by locating Hemmings at this pivotal moment, we may tend to the haunts of history that also stand and speak here.

Jefferson's "original Rough draught," which was largely drafted at this site and shared with the Second Continental Congress on June 28, 1776, also included a later-deleted passage referring to slavery, in Jefferson's words, as a "cruel war against human nature itself." The full passage reads:

> *He [the King of England] has waged cruel war against human nature itself, violating its most sacred rights of life and liberty in the persons of a distant people who never offended him, captivating & carrying them into slavery in another hemisphere, or to incur miserable death in their transportation thither. This piratical warfare, the opprobrium of INFIDEL Powers, is the warfare of the CHRISTIAN king of Great Britain. Determined to keep open a market where MEN should be bought & sold, he has prostituted his negative for suppressing every legislative attempt to prohibit or to restrain this execrable commerce. And that this assemblage of horrors might want no fact of distinguished die, he is now exciting those very people to rise in arms among us, and to purchase that liberty of which he has deprived them, by murdering the people on whom he also obtruded them: thus paying off former crimes committed against the LIBERTIES of one people, with crimes which he urges them to commit against the LIVES of another.*[2]

These are words the Second Continental Congress removed from the final version in the days leading up to July 4. This deleted passage is among the central contradictions that were not Jefferson's alone to hold—they are also the contradictions that run under and through our nation today. They are part of an unreconciled past that continues to reinforce systems of injustice, haunt our present, and influence our individual and collective futures.

It is said that Jefferson sat silently as debate swirled among a group that included those who claimed ownership over other people and fought to remove this language. While you can read Jefferson's original drafted words in esteemed locations such as the Library of Congress, the changes made in the declaration's formation continue to inform our history today. While Jefferson's words that "all men are created equal" constantly echo in the civic imagination of the United States, this deleted phrase conveying enslavement as a "cruel war against human nature itself" remains elusive unless you know where to look.

This book aims to make room for a fuller history by revisiting the site of the Declaration House, mapping it onto the city and nation, past and present, as a way to tend to our democracy today. The mission of Monument Lab—to advance justice by reimagining monuments as places of learning, healing, and belonging—led us here. The work of diving into the layered history of the Declaration House was a coalitional effort, and art remains at the core of this historical endeavor.

In 2022, Monument Lab began partnering with artist Sonya Clark, Independence National Historical Park, and later, the Thomas Jefferson Foundation, the nonprofit that owns and operates Monticello, as well as other civic partners, to produce a temporary, exterior-facing installation at Declaration House. Clark is a celebrated visual artist who summons historical reflection through participation and collaboration. Responding to the fact that there are no known historical images of Hemmings, Clark worked with the Thomas Jefferson Foundation's Monticello and its Getting Word African American History Department to document the eyes of Hemmings's collateral descendants and others who are related to the more than four hundred people enslaved at Monticello, including those biologically related to Jefferson.

In her resulting artwork, "The Descendants of Monticello," Clark juxtaposed contemporary video portraits of the eyes of living descendants with eyes drawn from photographs of descendants in Monticello's archives to form a multichannel video installation facing the intersection of Seventh and Market Streets. With this artwork, the historic house came to life through a monumental montage of blinking eyes that engaged passersby. Visitors to this temporary exterior installation were also invited to respond to the project's central prompt—What does the Declaration of Independence mean to you today?—with hand-drawn responses at a Welcome Station in the courtyard of the house.

In the United States and beyond, the house is a significant container of history. House museums are prominent sites where we access, interpret, and embody the past. There are more than fifteen thousand house museums in the United States, including a number of prominent sites that conjure historic Philadelphia.[3] Such houses are sites in which we are instructed, often from a young age, how to remember, who to remember, and how to balance the pride and pains of our past with a healing and hopeful sense of the future. Architects and preservationists approach this task in a number of ways. Some approach the exercise, as Svetlana Boym notes, as a "restorative" effort, with the goal of not only indexing the past but reenacting it. Others take the alternate "reflective" approach, accounting for gaps, fragments, and incomplete aspects.[4]

Monticello, the only house on a U.S. coin and Jefferson's former plantation, is often seen—in the national imagination—as a city on a hill itself. Although construction of the neoclassical structure began in 1769, the house was not considered complete until 1809, although Jefferson never stopped refining the interior and exterior. Ultimately it was abandoned before being purchased and preserved by naval officer Uriah Levy and his family. But the preservation led by the Levy family is only a fragment of the story; the fact is, the majority of the inhabitants of this land were Black families who made an imprint on this space for generations.

When it comes to Black history in the United States, the inequities of representation in the historic landscape are staggering. Of the ninety-five thousand sites listed on the National Register of Historic Places, only 2 percent focus on Black American life. This issue is not only empirical but one that speaks to the heart of the vexed relationship between public memory and citizenship in the United States, often played out through our monument landscape. It summons a reading not just of who and what is present in history's often spotlighted narratives but of the absences and silences as intentional. In this book, we follow forebearers, including Danielle Allen, Annette Gordon-Reed, Nikole Hannah-Jones, Clint Smith, Lucia C. Stanton, and

Salamishah Tillet, in their groundbreaking work with archives and historic fragments to recover the stories of enslaved people, including Hemmings, amid the histories of Jefferson and Monticello.[5] We also are guided by Toni Morrison's notion of literary archeology: "On the basis of some information and a little bit of guesswork, you journey to a site to see what remains were left behind and to reconstruct the world that these remains imply." This "guesswork" or "rememory" involves honoring historical inquiry while bridging gaps with artistic acts of recovery.[6]

Hemmings embodies the dualities of this nation. He was born enslaved and later gained his freedom. The record of his life is scant, sifted through mountains of materials penned by Jefferson, although a record of his own hand appears in a relatively newfound archival record (which is discussed in Andrew M. Davenport's essay "Robert Hemmings's Declaration of Independence"). His family members—some of them well known, such as his sister Sally and his brothers Peter and James—have been the focus of historical debate, discovery, and discourse. Robert was not lost to history, to be clear, with prominent mentions in historical accounts of the Declaration House and Monticello. Still, he has been either a footnote in the stories of founding freedom in Philadelphia or absent from the narrative altogether. The Monument Lab installation at Declaration House, a form of reparative public art envisioned with Sonya Clark, steps in where prevailing methods of collecting, retaining, and commemorating history fail. "The Descendants of Monticello" mobilizes creative methods rooted in illuminating the lives and livingness of descendants to honor what we cannot know while attempting to recuperate stories ready to be told.

While historians have gone to extraordinary efforts to recover any trace of the lives, thoughts, and full humanity of enslaved people and their families, they still must contend with the gaps in the record and presentation. Even the Hemmingses, one of the most documented enslaved families in U.S. history, are recounted with a fraction of the documents and archival materials available for many other historical figures, which compounds the challenge faced in historical efforts to see the world through their eyes.

Declaration House is Monticello's shadow house, a cipher in which to grapple with the origins and evolutions of U.S. democracy. Moving Robert Hemmings, as well as the many families and people enslaved at Monticello, to the center of this story reveals deeper insights into our still-emergent nation. In doing so, we are reminded of other under-spotlighted stories in Philadelphia, a birthplace of freedom and repression, abolition and dispossession. For example, just ten years before Jefferson's and Hemmings's time in the city, one in six Philadelphia homes housed at least one enslaved person. Likewise, outside those walls, free and enslaved people of African descent made homes, created networks of care and escape, and contended with the forces of repression in the cradle of liberty.

Jefferson is one of the most monumentalized figures in the U.S. commemorative landscape.[7] Retelling the story of the Declaration of Independence with Robert Hemmings at its center does not threaten to erase these other, better-known histories. Rather, this project contributes to a richer history of the worlds these men inhabited and, consequently, a richer sense of the contingencies that shaped their actions.

As we enter our nation's 250th year, the *Declaration House* project is a record of an experiment in its own right—to treat a historic site that was largely inactive as a space of vital and courageous storytelling, inspiring novel discussions centering healing, regeneration, and responsibility in the present. We also see this story, like that of our nation and its founding documents, as one that continues to echo—to demand persistence, attunement, and vigilance alongside ongoing, creative attempts at understanding.

This book gathers essays, poems, conversations, and artworks related to "The Descendants of Monticello" and the *Declaration House* project to assess and explore the Declaration of Independence, its authors, contributors, constituents, and all of us as works in progress. Whether you bring your copy with you on a trip to Independence National Historical Park in Philadelphia, consider it as an addendum to time spent at Monticello outside Charlottesville, or examine its ideas and artwork anywhere in the world, this book is about navigating geographies of freedom and belonging. We invite readers to consider Clark's artwork and the written offerings in the book as lenses to at once access the past, grapple with the present, and reach toward a freer and more just future. We carry forward with these premises: The more we tell our full history as a country, the more we heal our wounds. The more we break patterns of generational harm. The more we chip away at gaps formed by history. The more we can innovate and live with one another with grace and with possibility.

We went looking for Robert Hemmings and found America.

## NOTES

1. Thomas Jefferson, "Declaration of Independence," Thomas Jefferson Foundation, https://www.monticello.org/declaration/.

2. Thomas Jefferson, "Transcript of the Rough Draft of the Declaration of Independence," Thomas Jefferson Foundation, https://www.monticello.org/thomas-jefferson/jefferson-s-three-greatest-achievements/the-declaration/transcript-of-the rough-of-the-declaration/.

3. Susan R. Orr, "Historic House Museum Sustainability in the 21st Century: Paths to Preservation" (Ph.D. diss., Seton Hall University, 2011), https://scholarship.shu.edu/cgi/viewcontent.cgi?article=1660&context=dissertations#:~:text=Today%2C%20Americans%20still%20cherish%20the,museums%20in%20the%20United%20States.

4. Svetlana Boym, *The Future of Nostalgia* (New York: Basic Books, 2001), xviii.

5. Danielle Allen, *Our Declaration: A Reading of the Declaration of Independence in Defense of Equality* (New York: Liveright Publishing Corporation, 2015); Annette Gordon-Reed, *The Hemingses of Monticello: An American Family* (New York: Norton, 2008); Nikole Hannah-Jones, "Democracy," in *The 1619 Project: A New Origin Story*, eds. Nikole Hannah-Jones, Caitlin Roper, Ilena Silverman, and Jake Silverstein (New York: One World, 2021); Clint Smith, *How the Word Got Passed: A Reckoning with the History of Slavery across America* (New York: Little, Brown, 2021); Lucia C. Stanton, *"Those Who Labor for My Happiness": Slavery at Thomas Jefferson's Monticello* (Charlottesville: University of Virginia, 2012); Salamishah Tillet, *Sites of Slavery: Citizenship and Racial Democracy in the Post-Civil Rights Imagination* (Durham, NC: Duke University Press, 2012).

6. Toni Morrison, "Site of Memory," in *Out There: Marginalization and Contemporary Cultures*, ed. Russell Ferguson (New York: New Museum of Contemporary Art, 1990); Toni Morrison, *Beloved* (New York: Plume, 1987), 38; and Toni Morrison, "I Wanted to Carve Out a World Both Culture Specific and Race-Free," *Guardian*, August 8, 2019, https://www.theguardian.com/books/2019/aug/08/toni-morrison-rememory-essay.

7. Monument Lab, *The National Monument Audit*, 2021, https://monumentlab.com/audit.

# Editors' Note

This book compiles the work of multiple authors, and the use of terminology reflects the variances of their different scholarly, historical, and artistic approaches. The editors use the term *enslaved person* to refer to someone held in bondage, as opposed to the humanity-challenged word *slave*. Following the emergent research of the Getting Word African American History Department at Thomas Jefferson's Monticello, the spelling of Robert Hemmings's name, which differs from that of some of his relatives, reflects the way he signed the 1812 Richmond City Hustings Court marriage bond of his daughter, Elizabeth Hemmings, to William Scott; this document shows the only surviving instance of his signature and handwriting known to the historical record.

# DECLARATION HOUSE

# A Prayer for Robert Hemmings

Husnaa Haajarah Hashim

Through filtered light upon the gate, remember he had eyes
We reflect on the slow interior memory's eyes.

Stored material in each retina awakens us
Beyond and before. We see the world with energy eyes.

Memory is the interior. Sphere melts into sphere
Forgetting our nation's history? Better we use our eyes.

We carry the memories of all our peoples' people
Sunlight shifts, and we feel a synergy of eyes.

Foolish memory indeed swells enough to embody
A footnote that expands into identity, their eyes.

Memory floats back and repeats its offering of sight
We rest shopping bags and jugs of juice. Remedy with eyes.

Stroke of the signature an archival blessing
As we focus on a lineage. Forever be their eyes.

# Robert Hemmings's Declaration of Independence

Andrew M. Davenport

During the late spring and early summer of 1776, Thomas Jefferson drafted the Declaration of Independence in rented lodgings on the second floor of a three-story brick home on the southwest corner of Seventh and High (later called Market) Streets in Philadelphia.[1] He was not alone at the time of the nation's founding; Jefferson's fourteen-year-old enslaved valet, Robert Hemmings, likely slept in the garret or the hallway outside his bedroom.[2] What did the Declaration of Independence mean to the young Hemmings?

Hemmings's ties to Jefferson and his family reveal what historian Annette Gordon-Reed calls "the infinitely strange, but still in some ways familiar, world of slavery."[3] Born in Charles City County, Virginia, in 1762, Hemmings was the eldest son of Elizabeth Hemings and her owner, John Wayles, an attorney, planter, and slave trader.[4] As an enslaved person, Hemmings's status as the firstborn son of this relationship, which eventually produced five other children, meant nothing legally.[5] It was Jefferson, who married Wayles's daughter Martha, and his two brothers-in-law, not Robert or his Hemings siblings, who inherited Wayles's fortune after his death in 1773.[6] Jefferson inherited 135 enslaved people, including his wife's half-siblings, which vaulted him into the uppermost strata of colonial Virginian society.[7] Just weeks after Wayles's death, Jefferson paid a tailor "for cutting out clothes for Bob," who soon assumed the trusted position of valet.[8] So began Hemmings's daily association with Jefferson until the latter left for France as minister plenipotentiary eleven years later.[9]

Unlike most enslaved people who were barred from literacy, Hemmings could read and write.[10] This advantage, coupled with the fact that Hemmings was his wife's half-brother, likely motivated Jefferson to assign Hemmings to the valet position.[11] Hemmings's literacy would have been a skill that Jefferson could rely on.[12] Indeed, at the outset of the Second Continental Congress in 1775, Jefferson planned for Hemmings to spend considerable time with him in Philadelphia. That October, Jefferson contracted Dr. William Shippen, who had inoculated Jefferson against smallpox nine years earlier, to inoculate Hemmings, who then had to be lodged and nursed for four weeks of convalescence.[13] One wonders about the thoughts that coursed through the young Hemmings's mind during that period as his body protected itself against a dreaded disease that was particularly contagious in Philadelphia's urban environment. Once he recovered, Hemmings resumed his duties attending to Jefferson, who, beginning on June 11, 1776, busied himself with drafting the document that created the United States.[14]

On June 28, 1776, Jefferson submitted what he called an "original Rough draught" to the Congress.[15] After days of debates and edits, the Congress adopted the Declaration of Independence, which formally separated the United States from Great Britain, on July 4.[16] The final draft contained the immortal phrase "all men are created equal," but not Jefferson's original criticisms of slavery as "a cruel war against human nature itself."[17] The Congress determined that independence was its overarching goal and that "so monumental a change as the abolition of slavery could not be accomplished in a moment," historian Pauline Maier writes.[18]

Jefferson was far from the only critic of slavery then living in Philadelphia. He and Hemmings resided among free and enslaved African Americans who joined cause with allied white people, including Quakers, who comprised the city's abolitionists.[19] Hemmings doubtlessly witnessed and may have participated in conversations about slavery's injustices. There can be no doubt that Hemmings considered his own plight and that of his large family—his mother, siblings, and scores of cousins and extended relatives—who were enslaved on Jefferson's plantations in Virginia.

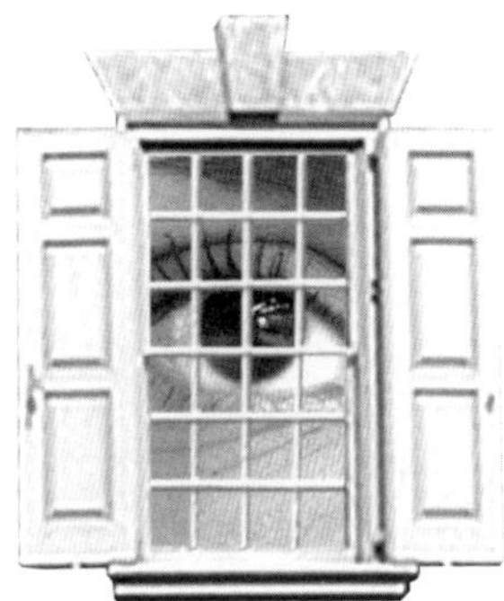

# DECLARATION HOUSE

this work, seeing yourself recognized. Now, I recognize these people too, as I see their eyes in the windows. Seeing yourself be seen. Seeing others see you. Witnessing your ancestors in your eyes, and just like that, this collapses this space and acknowledges the water that we are, essential, everywhere, cutting through the stone of history across time.

One other thing that was such a surprise to me in the artwork. Of course, we planned to use these big monitors in each of the windows of Declaration House to play the videos of the eyes. But when at night it became a lighthouse, a multi-eyed beacon, that was such a gift. As Earth turns away from the sun, the eyes of the descendants of Monticello light up Philadelphia. And the building, the Declaration House, falls away. The eyes are all you see. I didn't plan that; that's the serendipity. That's when the artwork is so much larger than me, me as the artist being the vessel that the artwork came through. But, of course, as I always say, this project happened in deep, deep collaboration with Getting Word, with the descendants, with Monument Lab, with MING Media—and then, in collaboration with every single person who walked by those streets. I think about how if everything that we've seen in our entire lives is held in our consciousness and therefore written and rewritten in our genetic code, then that means that artwork has the capacity to do that too. Everyone who has witnessed this artwork has actually been changed by it on some level. That's what we did together. We changed everybody who walked by. That's the power that I'm talking about and it's why artists must walk with responsibility.

**YW: What makes this project monumental? Because y'all are from D.C., you know a thing or two about monuments and what it means to live among them. I also know this living in Philadelphia. Some of our most important, our country's most important, monuments live in these places. "The Descendants of Monticello," for me, is a new kind of monument and a very necessary one. What do "The Descendants of Monticello" and the *Declaration House* project add to the monument landscape in our country?**

**GJW:** Our Black people, and women as well, have not been elevated as they should have as contributors to making America successful. And to me, this exhibition is alive. It's not static. It's not an equestrian or some big white man on a horse carrying a sword or looking down at Sacagawea, diminishing everyone but their own glory. That to me is really offensive. And I lived in Richmond when statues which were one hundred years old literally looked down on little Black boys and girls who really didn't know what those statues were. I know this because I talked to people in Richmond who grew up among those statues. They had no idea what those statues were, but they knew they were big white men looking down upon them and belittling them. "The Descendants of Monticello" is not so much a monument as a celebration. It's a celebration of who we are. It is alive. Those eyes are animated. Sonya pointed out that if you had a body attached to those eyes, it would be a colossus. It makes us as big as anyone who's been celebrated in the United States of America. Do you know how big a colossus is? Maybe bigger. Like the Statue of Liberty. And every American should have the experience of seeing those eyes—those animated eyes holding history accountable and holding all of us accountable for each other—and recognizing not just what Robert Hemmings and his descendants have done but what *we* have done.

**SC:** Gayle, I'm thinking about what you're saying about the Black and Brown children in Richmond walking by those monuments and thinking, "Those must be important people." But I'm also thinking about the white children who were walking by those monuments in Richmond and thinking, "We must be very important." And so I think about how white privilege and white supremacy doesn't exist unless it has its foot on the neck of somebody else. It's one thing to say, "We are," as Black and Brown people. And it's another thing for white folk to be like, "You know, we aren't!" Like this idea that "I must be smart because I'm white, I deserve to be wealthy"—that actually has to be undone. People don't relinquish power easily. The first time I heard someone say these words, it was you, Miss Yolanda Wisher: that Monument Lab defines a monument as "a statement of power and presence in public." So, who's in power, and who's present, and who's the public? And I love that definition because it does not talk to the supposed permanence of these Confederate statues that were erected. Some of them look like they're made of solid metal, and they're actually made cheaply and just seem large and impressive. You have to look up to them sitting on high plinths, right? Why does a monument require you to look up to it? Why is that how it's deriving its power? With "The Descendants of Monticello," what we were doing together is claiming power, making presence, and addressing the public. That was the assignment, and I think we did it.

I love these moments where you can tell when the eyes of the descendants are smiling. People are being human in their eyes. And all of that is held just on a large scale in the artwork. So much humanity is revealed in just this one part of the body, the eyes. And you think about how much of our bodies are denied. How much Black people are still policed for any little thing. We just recently said to Jordan Neely's family, "Your troubled son who was in a New York subway could be killed by a white man. And that's okay, because, you know, he was 'disturbing the peace.'" These examples are endless, but it's incredible how much policing there is around our bodies and yet how much humanity is expressed in just one single eye of each of the participants who were descendants of Monticello, who were part of this project, and how much humanity gets denied on a consistent level, and that this becomes this pushback, this resistance, this refusal to that denial as a monument, as a monument to freedom.

**GJW:** I was listening to everything you said, and it made me think of the day that all of you came with your team to Monticello to take the pictures of descendants and how excited everyone was and eager to participate. And the pride that we have in our ancestors and, to use your metaphor, how they have flowed through time with us and made us who we are. And I know that we're down to the last of this conversation, but before we finish, I just want to thank both of you and all who participated in this and making this project and engaging us in this project and allowing us to embrace who we are and who our ancestors were. What's so significant is that we love these people. Robert Hemmings is real for me. And Sally [Hemings]'s real. And Peter [Hemings]'s real. When I walk around Monticello, particularly when I'm in the space where James [Hemings] and Peter [Hemings] were, where they were cooking together, I feel them. They're real. I'm working on a book about Mom's family now, and I know these people. Mommy didn't know at least one set of her grandparents. She didn't know, but I know them.

**SC:** Oh, that's so beautiful.

**GJW:** And it's a remarkable journey. I'm just really pleased that I and my DNA cousins had a chance to bring these stories alive through your art, through the instrument of both of you, because we all made it possible. So, I just really appreciate it. And *they* appreciate it.

**SC:** It remains to date the piece that has changed me the most, and we, again, we did it together. There was an opportunity, and then we came together and realized that into something that honestly has changed me as the first public artwork I've ever made. Ever. And there was the trust that was required, shifts that were made, you know, because at first we were like, "Oh, we'll just use the Hemmings line of descendants." But just expanding that to include all the descendants of enslaved families at Monticello and feeling the power of the ancestors rush in, and we got that expanded feeling of love and camaraderie. Also, if someone asked me how many days we were at Monticello, I would answer, "Oh, I was there for months!" The kinship felt very real. And that's love. That's love and purposefulness. And that can only happen in true community. So, I'm really grateful to you. I'm going to start crying—but I'm really grateful.

**YW: My last question stems from thinking about how much this project has been about ancestry, how much it's influenced my thinking about my own ancestors and my reflections about them. I had originally wanted to ask you this question: "What kind of ancestor do you hope to be?" But because we are breaking the boundaries of time and linearity in this conversation, I'm asking y'all: "What kind of ancestor are you?" And what do you hope to do with your ancestor status?**

**SC:** I mean, I'd like to think, as I said before, that I'm adding to the ancestral archive, that I'm not harming it in any way. The archive is rich and full and has the good, the bad, and the ugly in it. My intent is to add to it in the good ways, but I am human, so I may falter. I think it's such a profound question that it's the kind of question that you want to ask yourself every day. And I actually would like to ask it of the people who are reading this conversation, to just leave it at, like, "What kind of ancestor are you?" Provocative questions mean that we're constantly in dialogue with the question, which means that we're constantly shifting and reevaluating and thinking. For me, that's also what the best artwork does. It doesn't provide an answer. It gives you a question to keep, to stay by your side, to hold and guide you. This question is something that will stay by my side. It's now going to be on my wall in my studio as this positive provocation of how to be in the world. So, I don't have an answer—I have a guide. I feel like it's a gift. And I'm just taking that gift in, receiving it, and doing my best by that gift.

**GJW:** I'm going to keep this really simple. This is Mom's birthday. And usually I get through Mom's birthday without shedding a tear. She was fabulous. She was kind of crazy, but she was fabulous—which you'll read about in my second book. But I wept this morning. I wept and I wept and I wept, and I could not turn it off. Because today, I miss her. And when you write, it's like—I mean, you guys are writers and artists, you know—you really get into these lives. In this case, it's not a memoir. It's about her. It's about her dad. But there's a lot of memory in it. I'm living her life over again. I'm living *her*. And when you ask what kind of ancestor I'd like to be, I just want to be. I want to be remembered the way my mom is remembered. I shared a picture of her with my girlfriends today. Mommy's kicking her legs up on the hood of somebody's car. I don't recognize the car or the people. She was maybe in her sixties, seventies. I'm looking at how she looks. I mean, she wasn't young—maybe my age, I don't know—but she's just leaning back on the car,

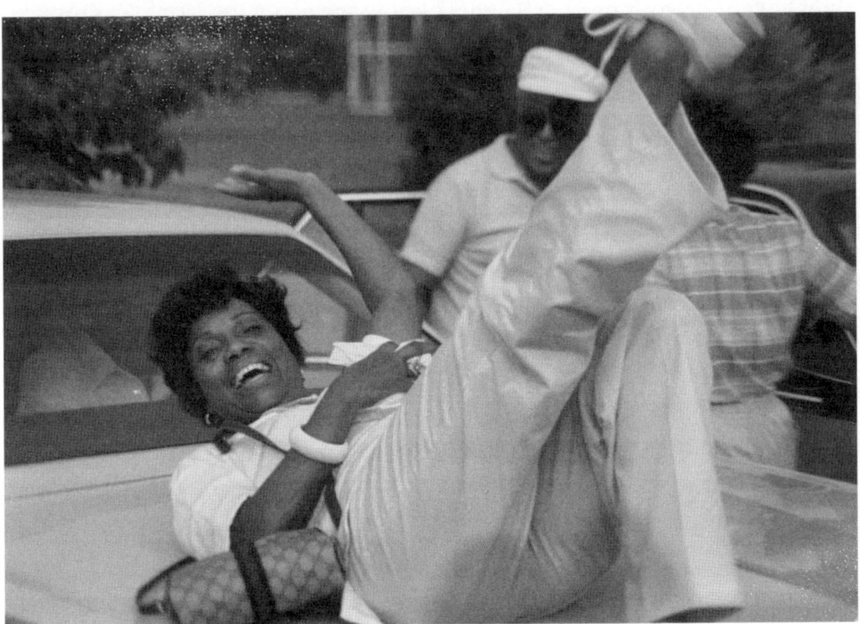

Gayle's mother, Theresa "Billye" Jessup.

kicking her legs up and laughing, and the guys are looking at her and laughing, and I'm thinking, "What a hoot." She was totally uninhibited. But if I can be remembered by the people who loved me, I'm happy. That's all the ancestor I need to be.

**SC:** So, first of all, you *do* make people happy. You're always funny. We're talking about some serious shit, and you're still funny. You still bring joy. And I love that about you. I also am thinking about how free your mother sounds like she was. The image that I have in my head is of her taking space. Yes, the legs up, and like that Nina Simone quote, "I'll tell you what freedom is to me: No fear!" So, the ancestor that I am, I hope, is someone who is free. Just working on freedom and taking this space of being free. And your image of your mother reminded me of my favorite image of my mother. Well, I have two, but this one in particular, when my mother was with her friends. She was probably a little younger than I am now. She was probably in her forties, early fifties, and she has her mouth wide open, her head tossed back, and she is laughing so hard that whenever I see the picture, I hear her laugh. She's so joyful and free and filled with being loved. That's what makes us keep going, right? I can see your mother, Gayle. I know she was cute. Mine was too and a character too.

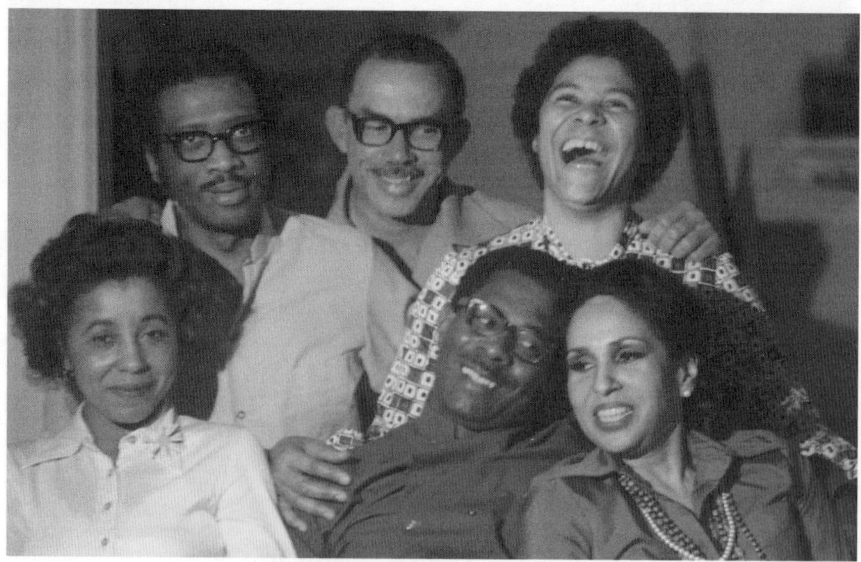

Sonya's mother, Lilleth Clark (*back row, far right*).

**GJW:** I can imagine.

**SC:** But I love that because they were the fullness of themselves. My mom did not take any shit from anybody. And she would decide if she liked you in the first two seconds of meeting you. And good luck crossing from one side to the other, because if she decided she didn't like you, that's that. And if she liked you, she fiercely held you tight. So, it sounds like they were so much themselves. And that's a kind of freedom, despite everything else. May we continue in this reclamation of freedom.

**GJW:** I love that. I love that. I love that freedom that they experienced and the reclamation of that. That's what we all need. That's where we're all going.

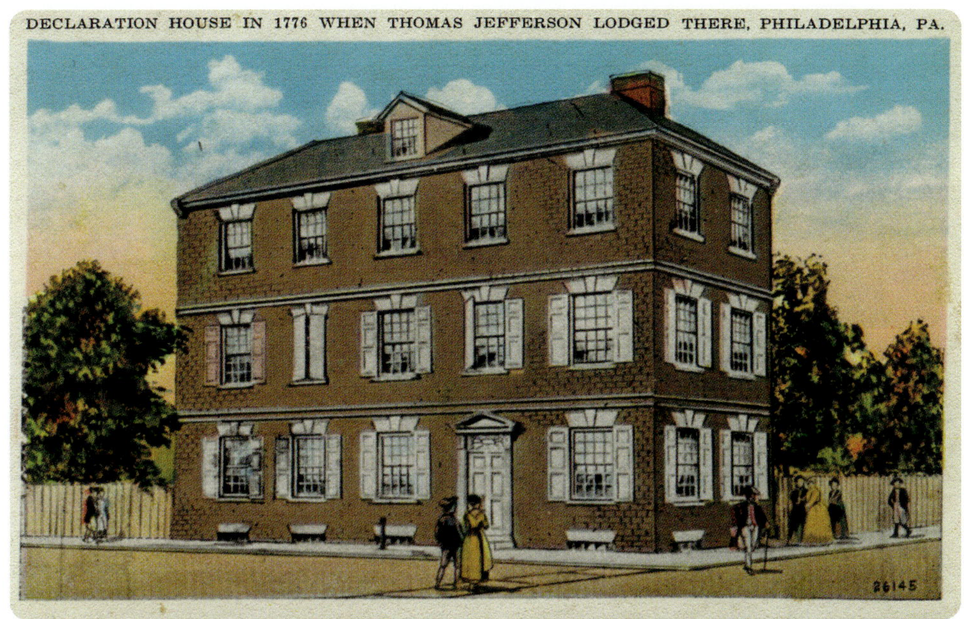


A postcard depicting what Declaration House would have looked like in 1776.

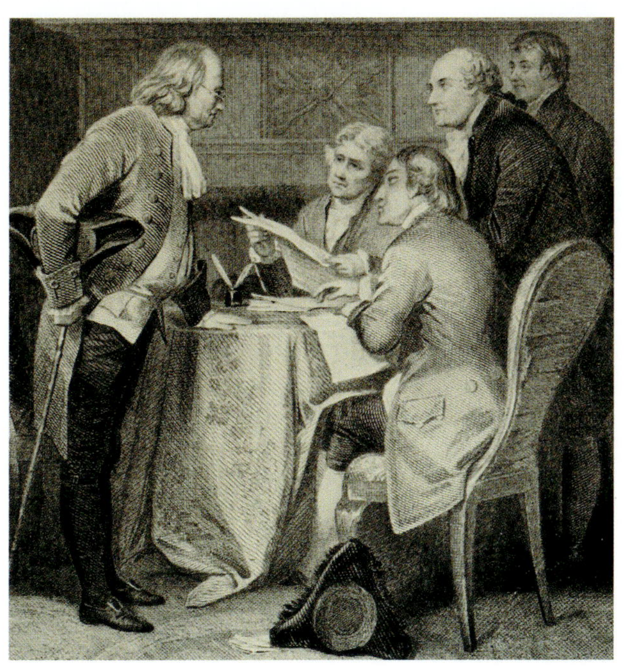

"A Conference as to the Declaration of Independence." Illustration depicting Thomas Jefferson reading the Declaration to members of the Continental Congress, including Dr. Benjamin Franklin, John Adams, Roger Sherman, and Robert R. Livingston, in his room in the house at no. 700 Market Street in June 1776. From Thomas Donaldson, *The House in Which Thomas Jefferson Wrote the Declaration of Independence*, 1898.

A Declaration by the Representatives of the UNITED STATES OF AMERICA, in General Congress assembled.

When in the course of human events it becomes necessary for one people to dissolve the political bands which have connected them with another, and to assume among the powers of the earth the separate and equal station to which the laws of nature & of nature's god entitle them, a decent respect to the opinions of mankind requires that they should declare the causes which impel them to the separation.

We hold these truths to be self-evident; that all men are created equal; that they are endowed by their creator with [equal] rights; that [inherent & inalienable], among these are life, liberty, & the pursuit of happiness; that to secure these rights, governments are instituted among men, deriving their just powers from the consent of the governed; that whenever any form of government becomes destructive of these ends, it is the right of the people to alter or to abolish it, & to institute new government, laying it's foundation on such principles & organising it's powers in such form, as to them shall seem most likely to effect their safety & happiness. prudence indeed will dictate that governments long established should not be changed for light & transient causes: and accordingly all experience hath shewn that mankind are more disposed to suffer while evils are sufferable, than to right themselves by abolishing the forms to which they are accustomed. but when a long train of abuses & usurpations [begun at a distinguished period, &] pursuing invariably the same object, evinces a design to reduce them under absolute Despotism, it is their right, it is their duty, to throw off such government, & to provide new guards for their future security. such has been the patient sufferance of these colonies; & such is now the necessity which constrains them to [expunge] alter their former systems of government. the history of the present king of Great Britain is a history of [unremitting] repeated injuries and usurpations, [among which, appears no solitary fact to contradict the uniform tenor of the rest, but all have] in direct object the establishment of an absolute tyranny over these states. to prove this, let facts be submitted to a candid world, [for the truth of which we pledge a faith yet unsullied by falsehood.]

Rough draft of the Declaration of Independence, written by Thomas Jefferson in 1776.

1794.

Dec. 14. sent by TMRandolph the £72-8-8 recieved yesterday from Milliner to James Lyle, this being one of the bonds destined towards the discharge of mine to Henderson McCaul & co.

16. pd for turkies 10/

20. pd Watson 4.D. assumed for do. to Peter 5.D. to Tom 4.D =13D

settled with Watson except blanks to be filled to some articles. agreed that making up lost time his year is up this day, & the new year is to begin on his return from Augusta.

23. received from Robert Hawkins £41-16 in discharge of his bond for that sum due the 14th. inst. this is one of the bonds destined for Henderson McCaul & co.

2 paid mr Bailey on account 30/

24. pd small exp. 1/6

pd Peter the 5.D. assumed for Watson.

executed a deed of emancipation for Bob. by the name of Robert Hemmings. he has been valued at £60. which Stras is to advance. inclosed to TMR. an order to recieve the £60. & to pay £41-16 of it to James Lyle for Henderson McCaul & co. instead of the £41-16 pd yesterday by Hawkins, which therefore I retain for other purposes. also to lodge 9. Dollrs with Colo. Harvie for J. Taylor to pay for a drill plough.

25. Small exp. 2.D.

26. do. 2.D.

sent by D. Carr to Thos. Walker £30-11-10. viz

for 7. mares to the Jack @ 2. guineas £19-12-0

abatement of 1/5 - - - - - . . 3-18-5

due to mrs Barclay - - - - - - . 15-13-7

due to T. Walker for a mule bought 15-

30-13-7

remains a balance still due him 1-9

30-11-10

gave D. Carr to purchase stockings for me 24/

27. gave Mr's Jamey & Billy 2. Doll. for their trips to Richmd with their waggon for my nail rod.

Thomas Jefferson's account book, 1791–1803, page 62.

*Know all men by these presents,* that we William Scott and Robert Hemmings

*are held and firmly bound unto* James Barbour *Governor or Chief Magistrate of the Commonwealth of Virginia, in the just and full sum of one hundred and fifty dollars; for the payment whereof, well and truly to be made to the said Governor or his successors, for the use of the said Commonwealth, we bind ourselves, our heirs, executors and administrators, jointly and severally, firmly by the presents. Sealed with our seals and dated this* 28th *day of* August *181*2

***The condition of the above obligation is such,*** that whereas a marriage is intended to be shortly had and solemnized between William Scott (Batchelor) above bound, and Elizabeth Hemmings (spinster) daughter of the said Ro: Hemmings. Now if there be no lawful cause to obstruct the said intended marriage, then the above obligation to be void, otherwise to remain in full force and virtue.

*Executed in presence of*

Th C Howard

William Scott (SEAL.)

Robert Hemmings (SEAL.)

Marriage between William Scott and Elizabeth Hemmings, August 28, 1812, Richmond City, Hustings Court Marriage Bonds, microfilm reel 123, film numbers 0094–0096.

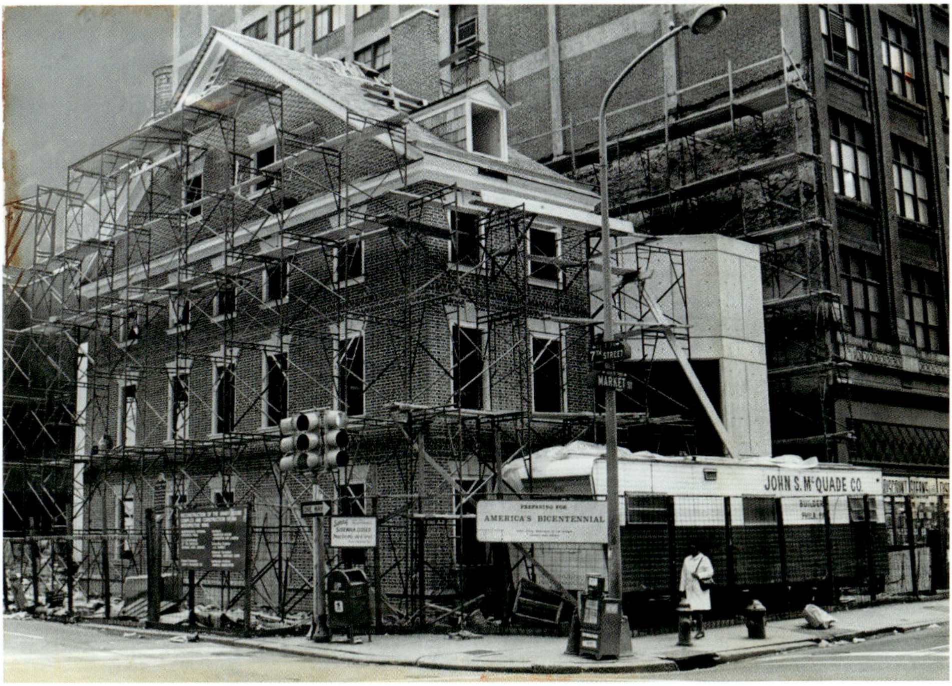

"When It All Began," Declaration House, Philadelphia, PA, 1975.

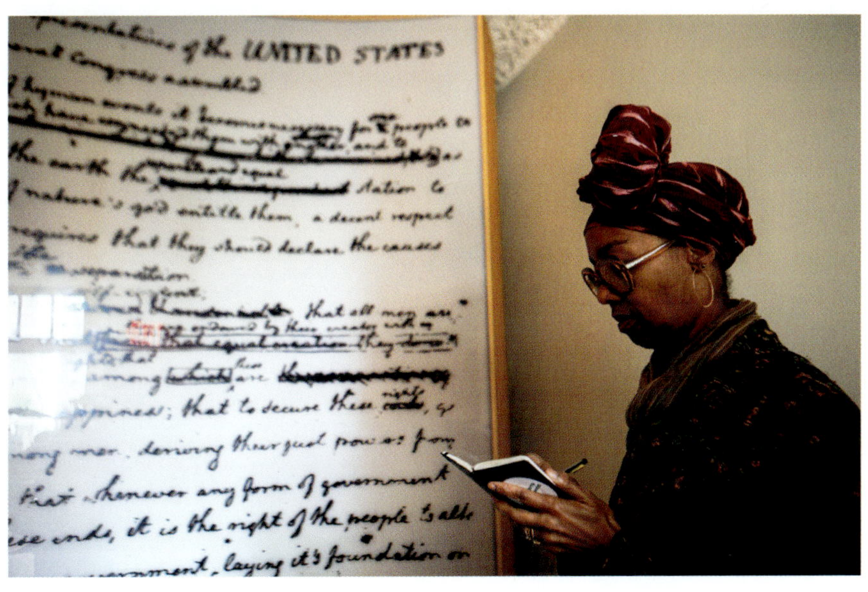


Sonya Clark site visit to Declaration House, Independence National Historical Park, Philadelphia, PA, 2023.

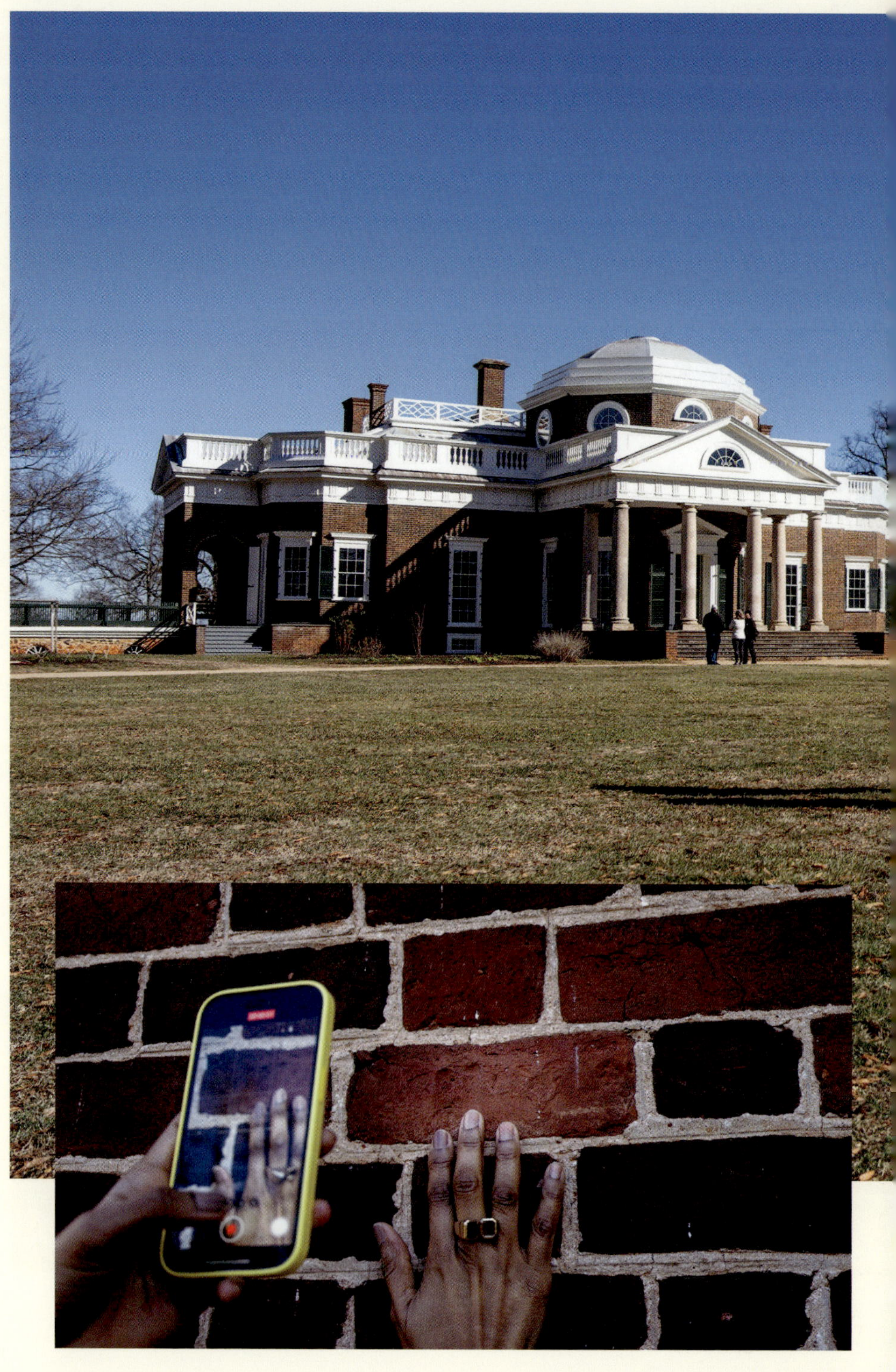

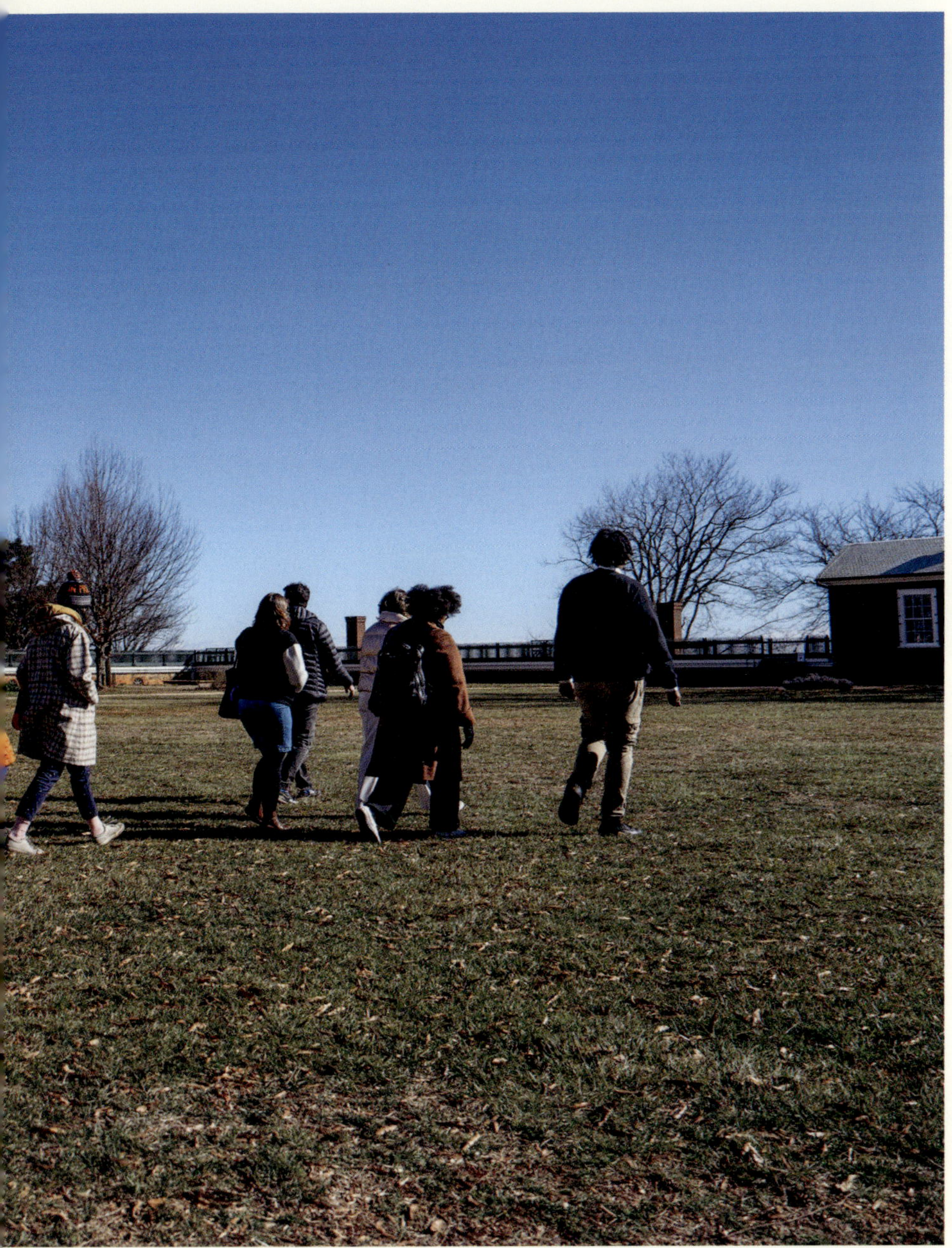

In 2024, *Declaration House* lead artist Sonya Clark traveled to Thomas Jefferson's historic estate, Monticello, with Monument Lab staff to explore the rich and complicated history of the site. There, they met with a group of Jefferson and Hemmings descendants who were photographed, interviewed, and later featured in Clark's artwork, "The Descendants of Monticello."

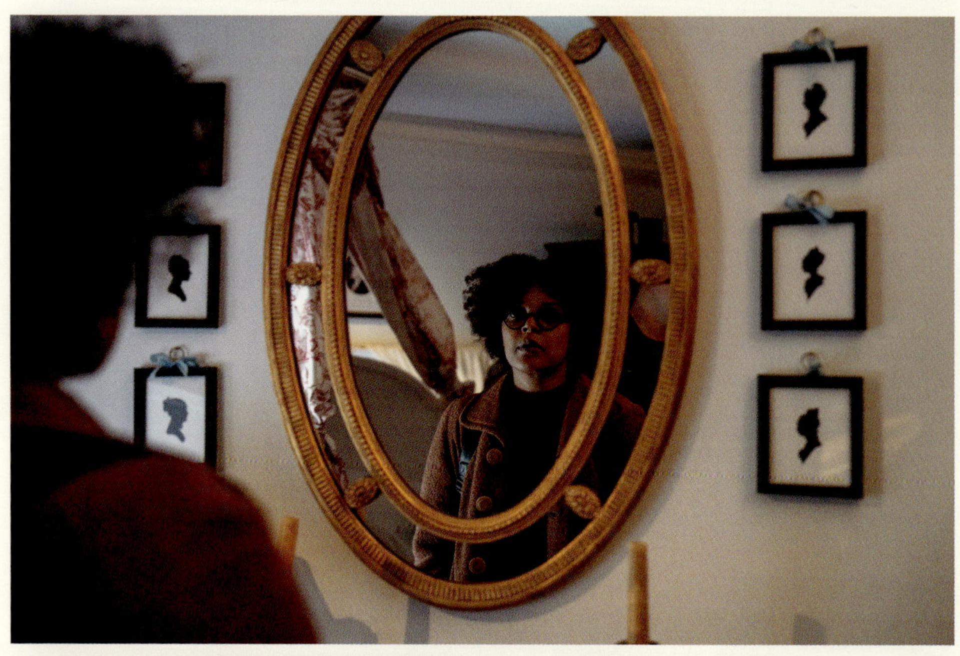

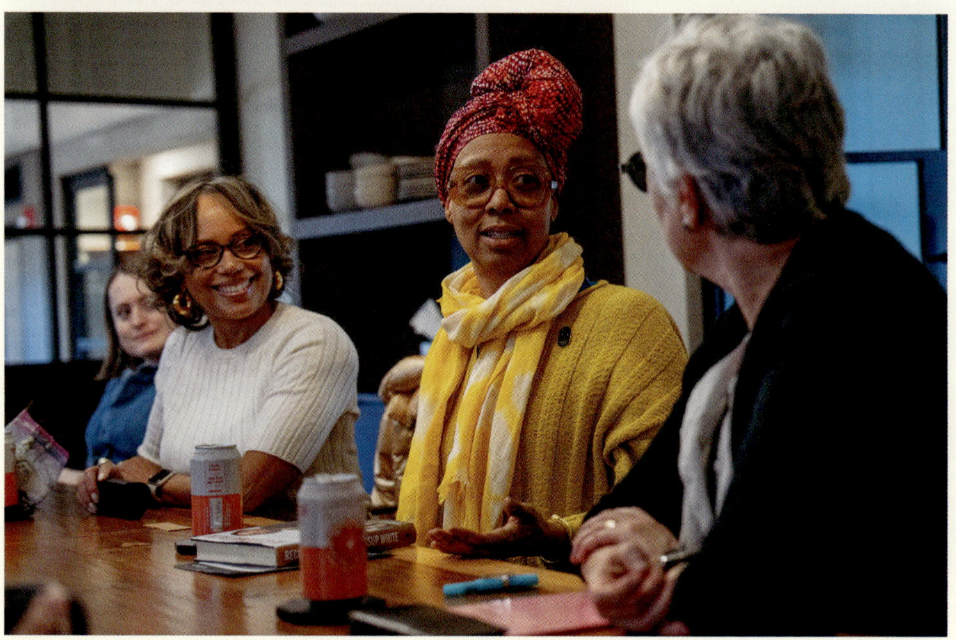

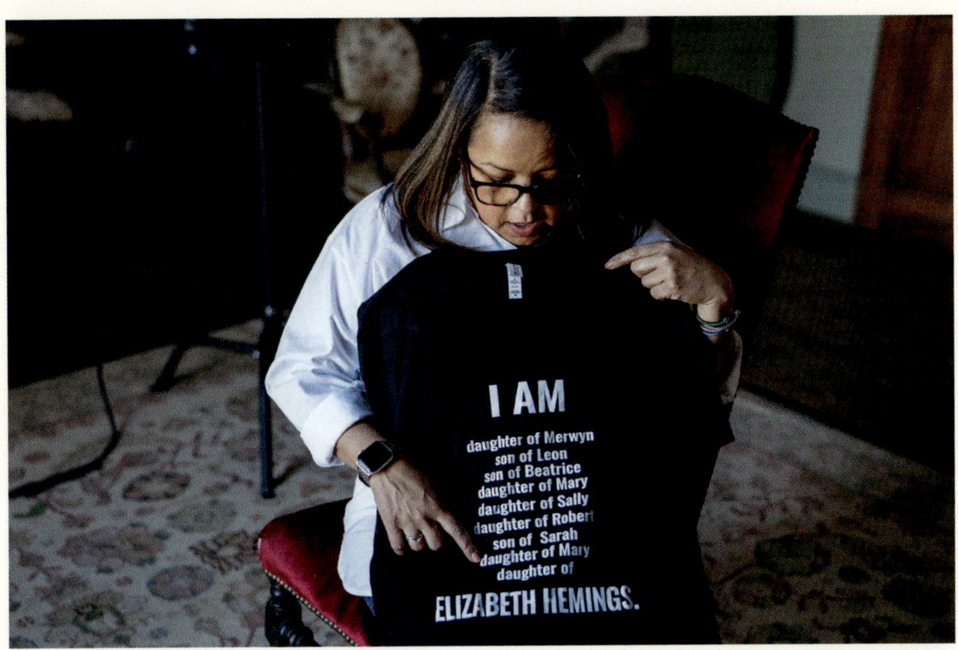
I AM
daughter of Merwyn
son of Leon
son of Beatrice
daughter of Mary
daughter of Sally
daughter of Robert
son of Sarah
daughter of Mary
daughter of
ELIZABETH HEMINGS.

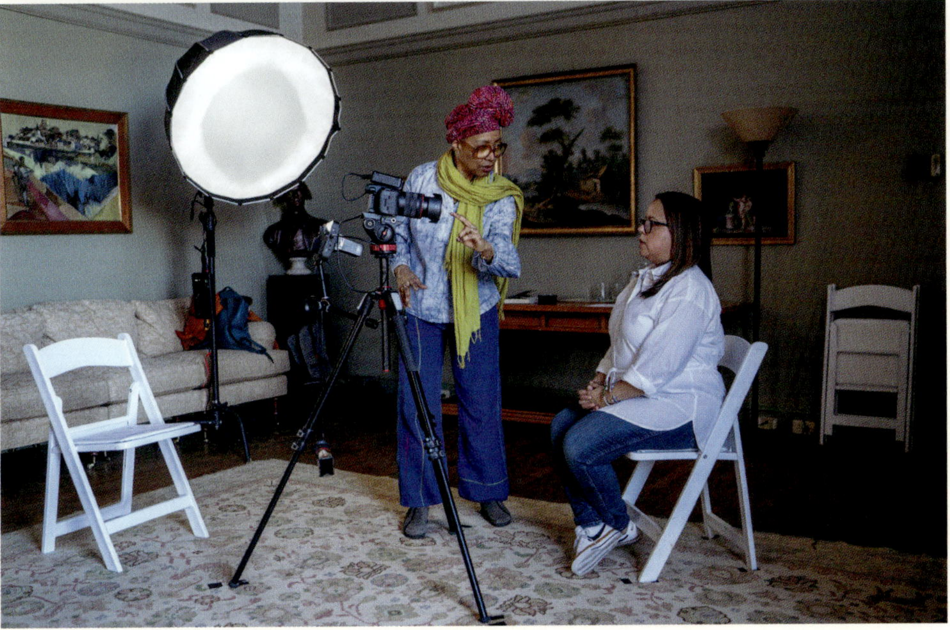

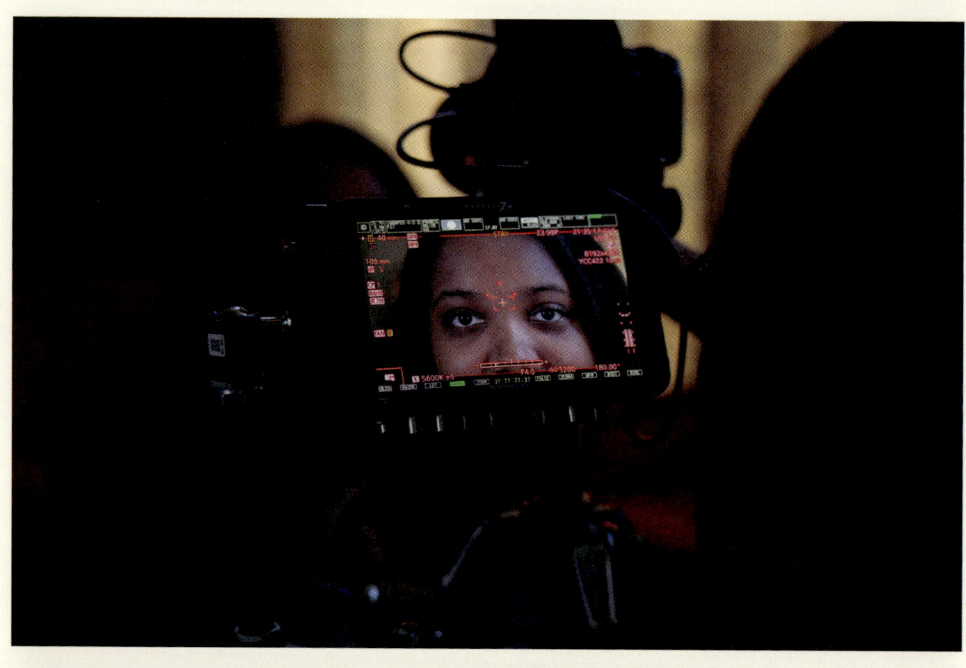

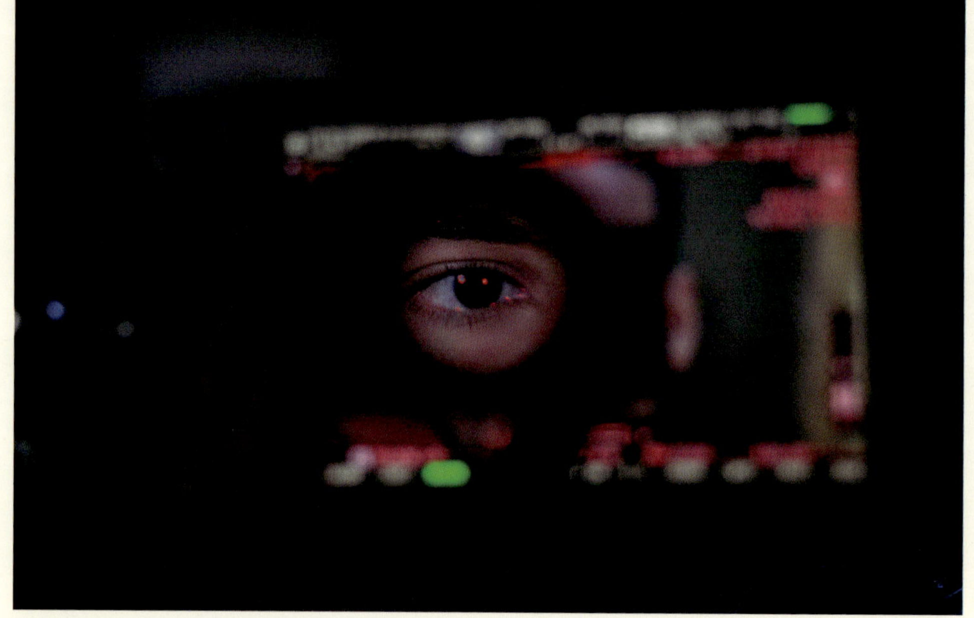

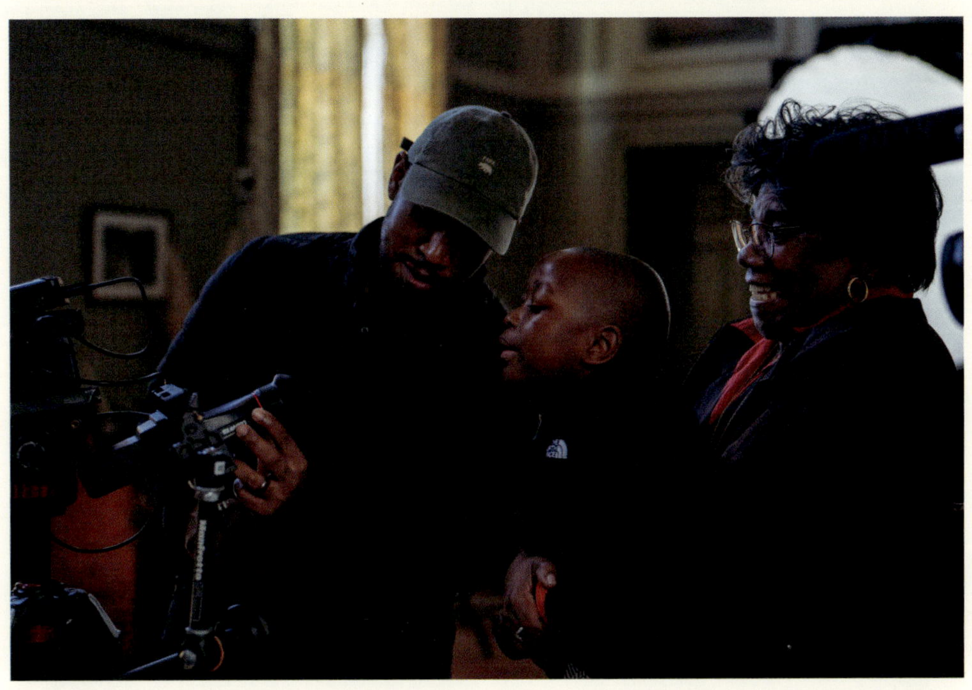

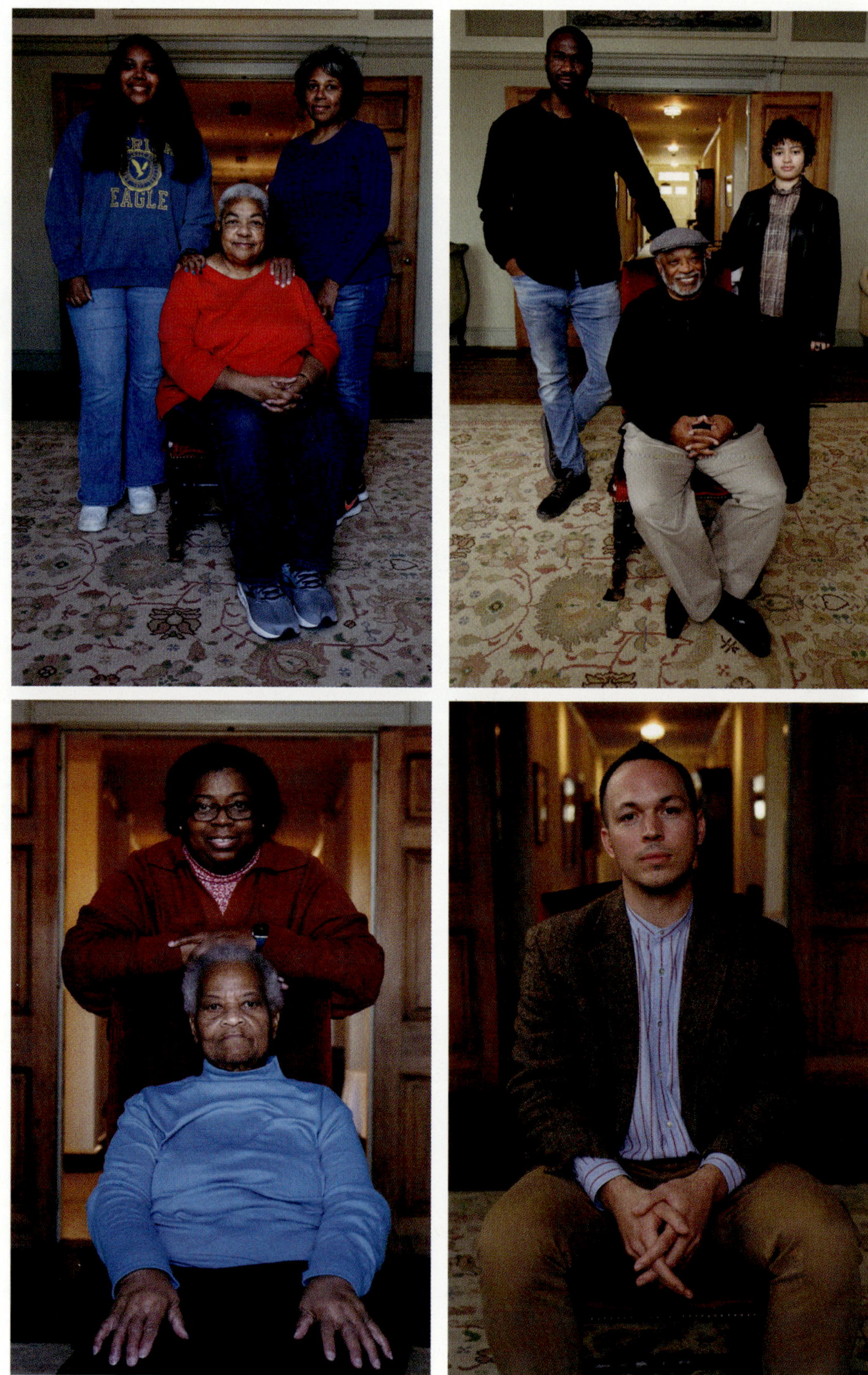
EAGLE

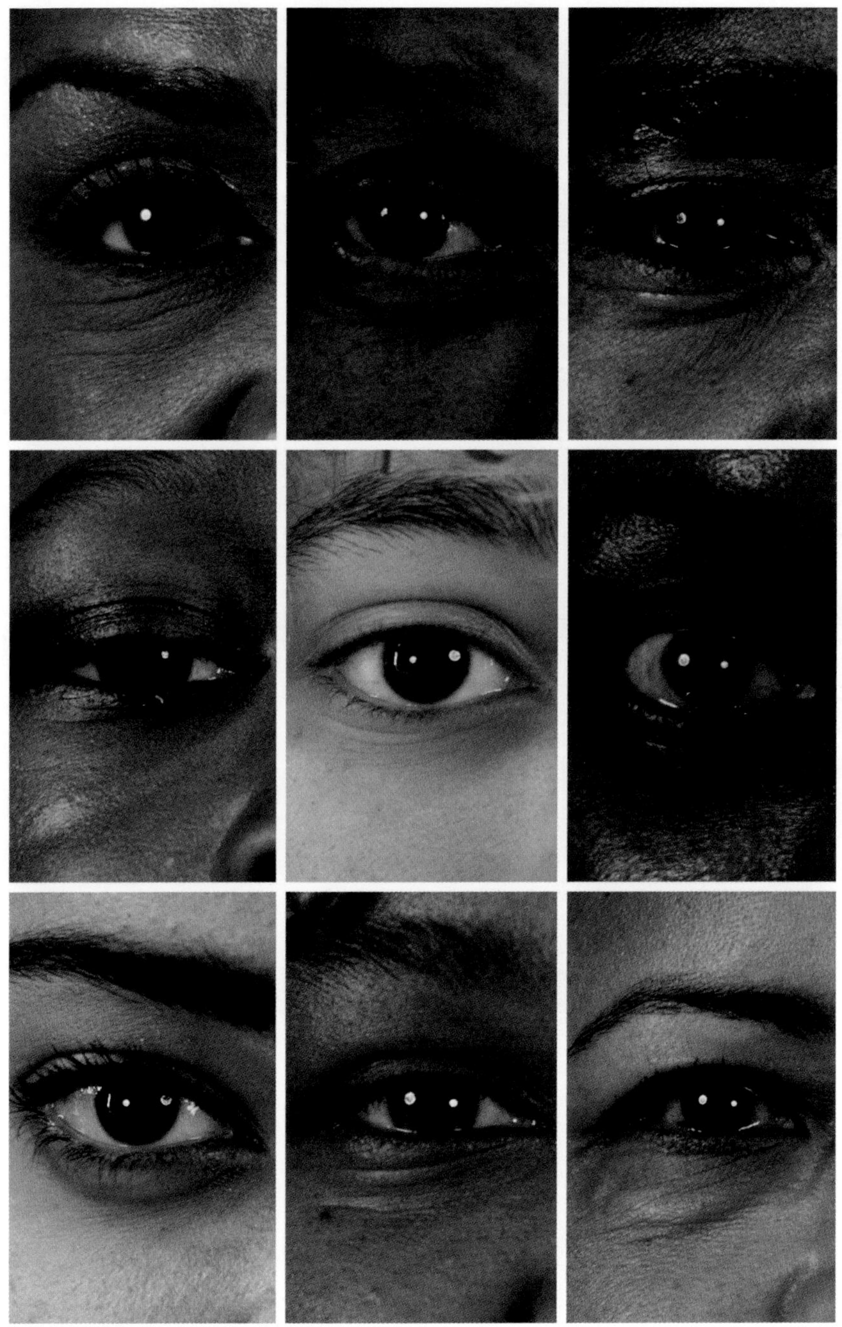

Edited eyes of descendants featured in Sonya Clark, "The Descendants of Monticello," *Declaration House*, Independence National Historical Park, Philadelphia, PA, 2024.

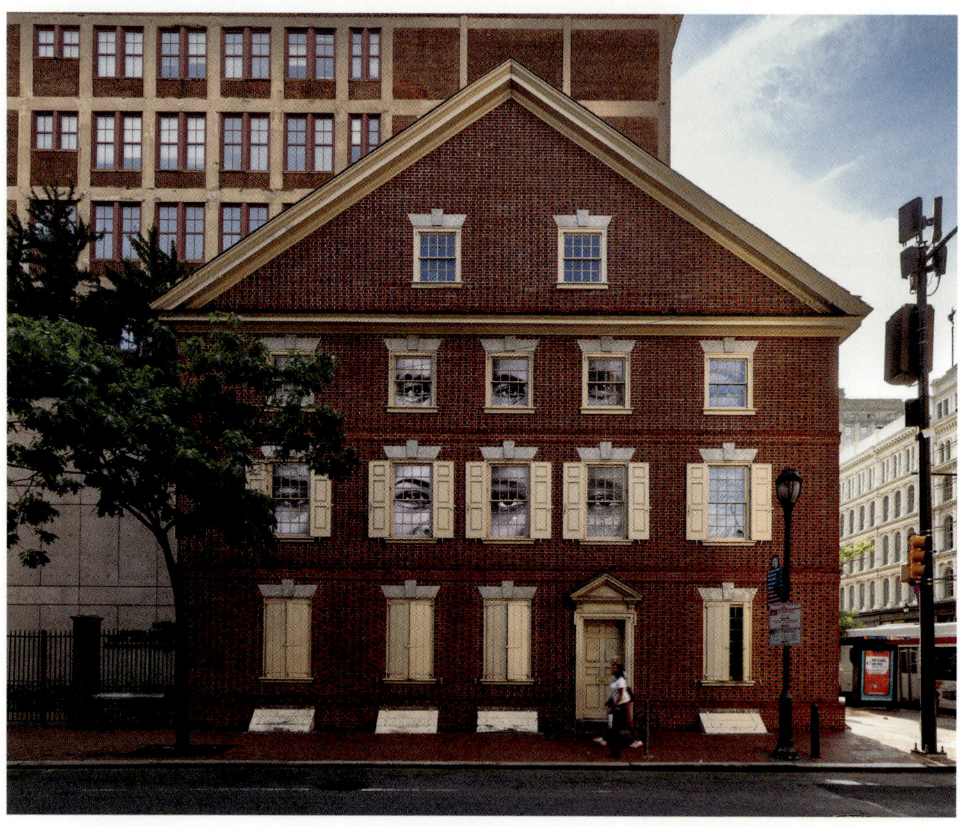

Situated at the corners of Seventh and Market Streets in Philadelphia, PA, in the windows of Declaration House, Sonya Clark's monumental montage "The Descendants of Monticello" captured the gaze of passersby and illuminated the block. Behind each window, the blinking eyes of Jefferson and Hemmings descendants, both living and ancestral, invited the public to examine the intertwined histories and legacies of the two men and their families.

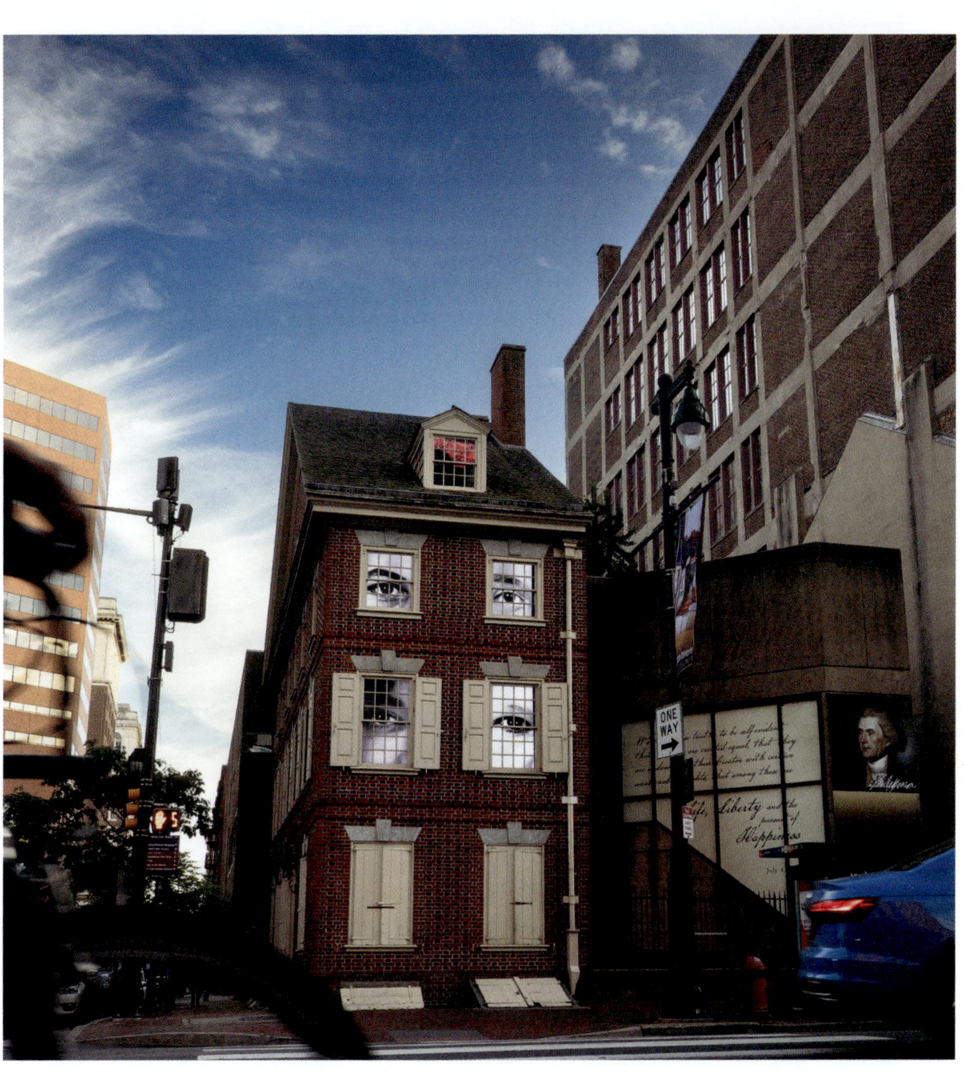
ONE WAY

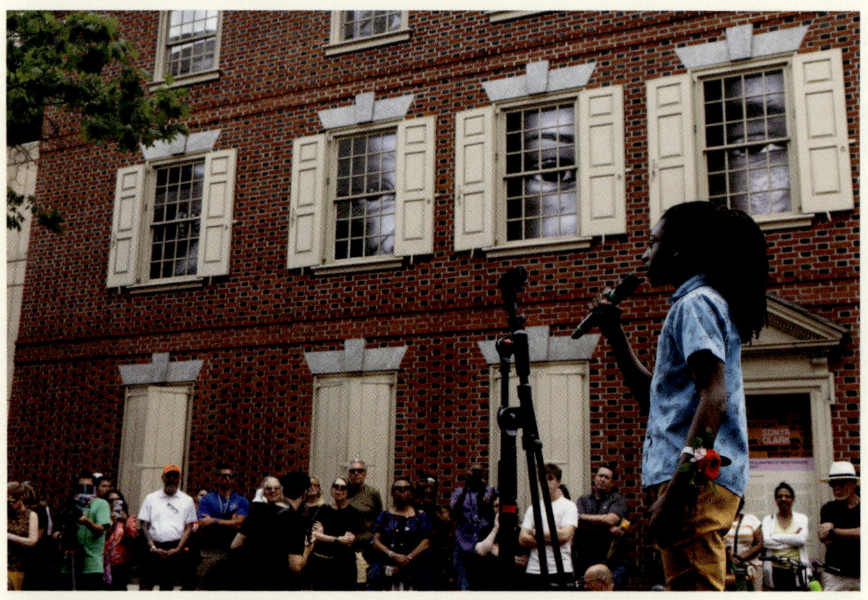

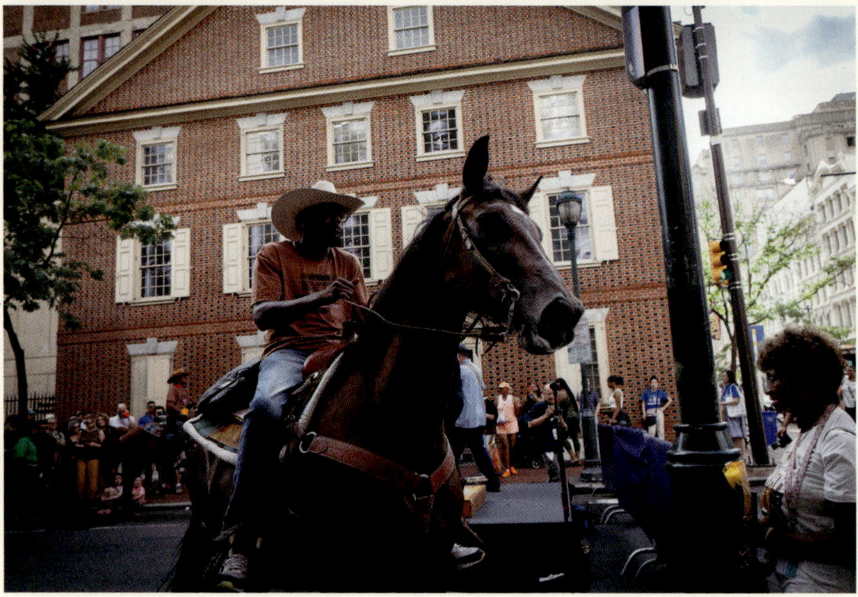

In the summer of 2024, the unveiling of Sonya Clark's "The Descendants of Monticello" was celebrated with a block party as part of Wawa Welcome America Festival. Through a curated speaking and performance program and welcome station, the event sought to activate Clark's artwork, honor the memory of Robert Hemmings, and invite the public to consider what the Declaration of Independence means to us today.

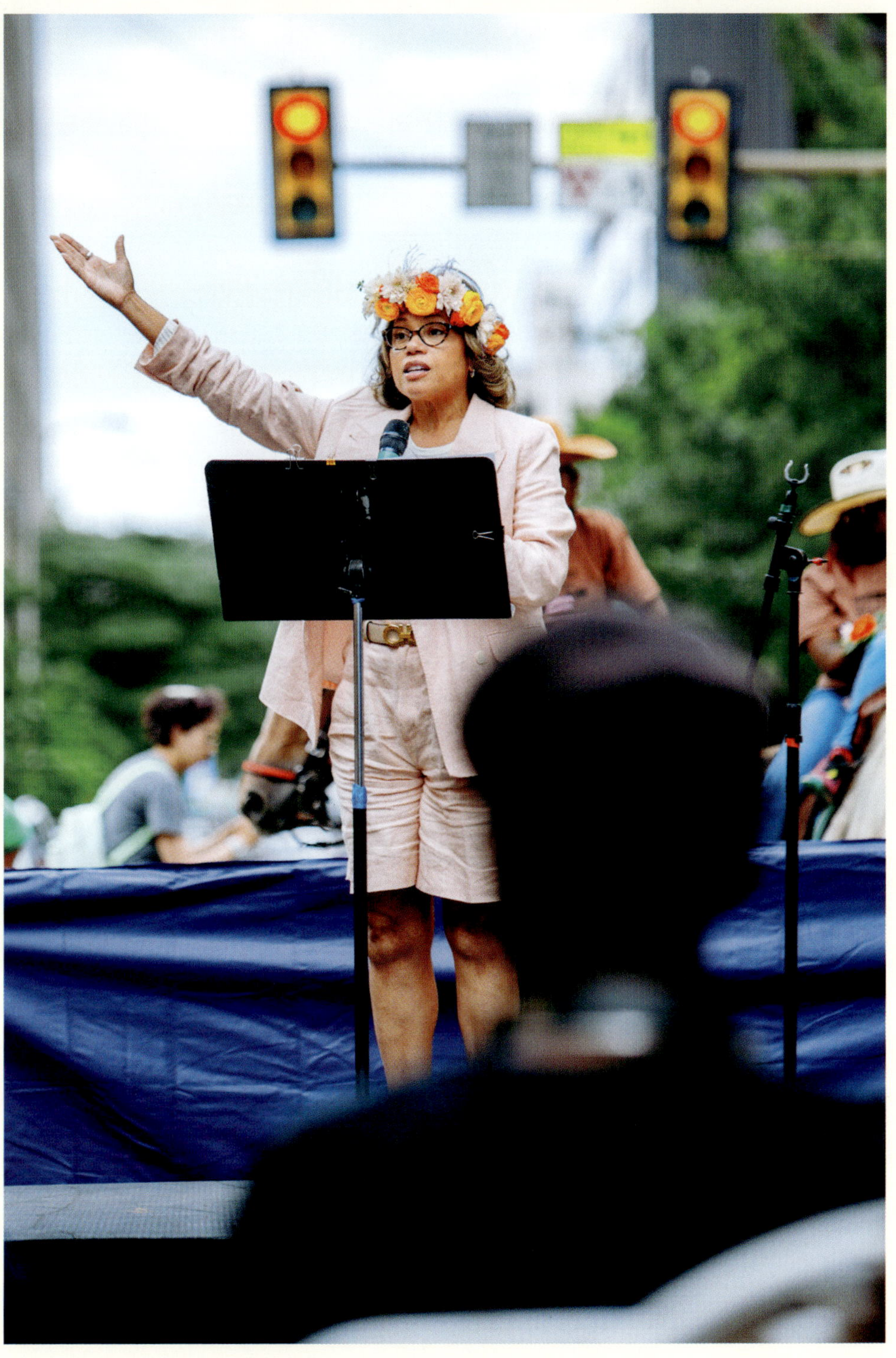

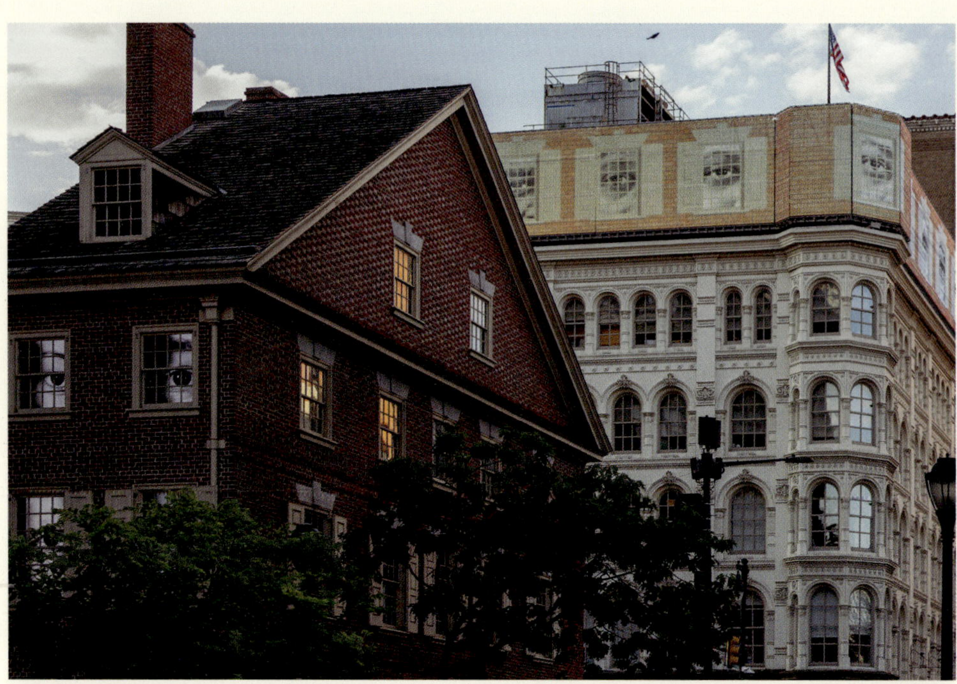

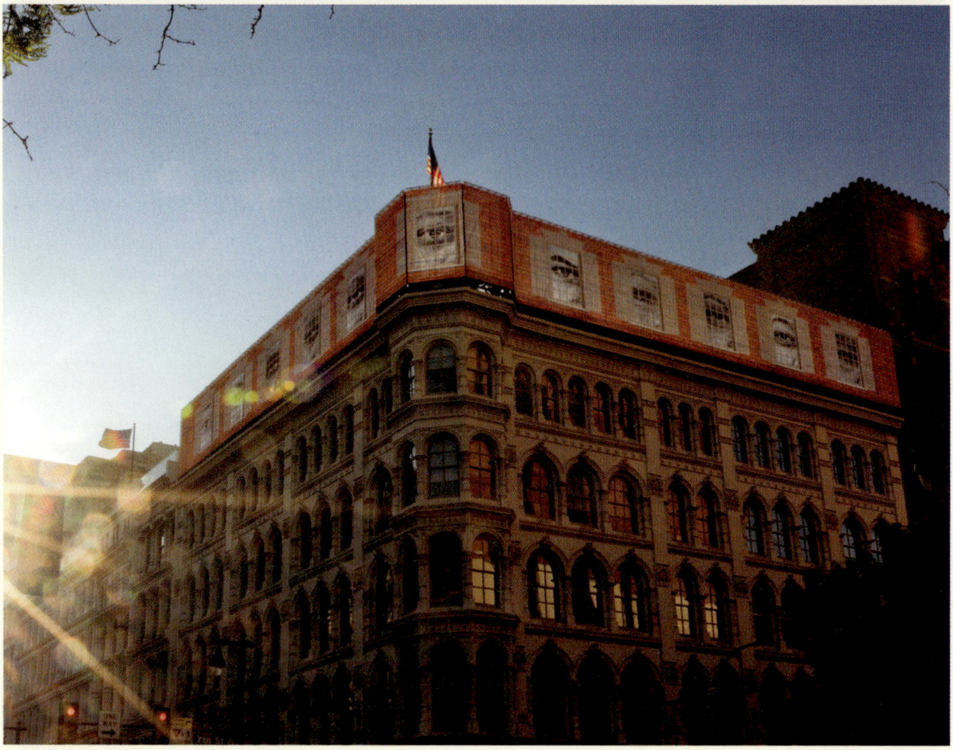

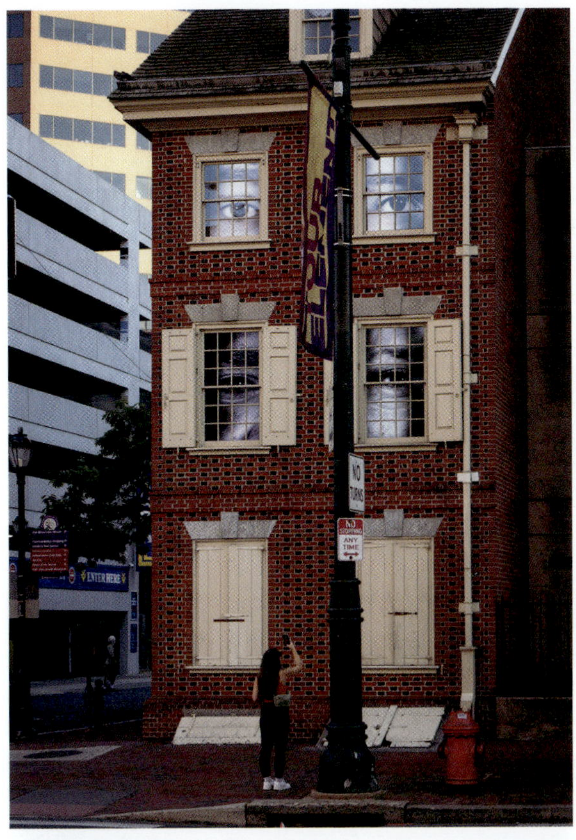


Juxtaposing the political climate of eighteenth-century America against the 2024 presidential election, Sonya Clark's "The Descendants of Monticello" became a lighthouse for America's uncertain future and a reflection of its haunted past.

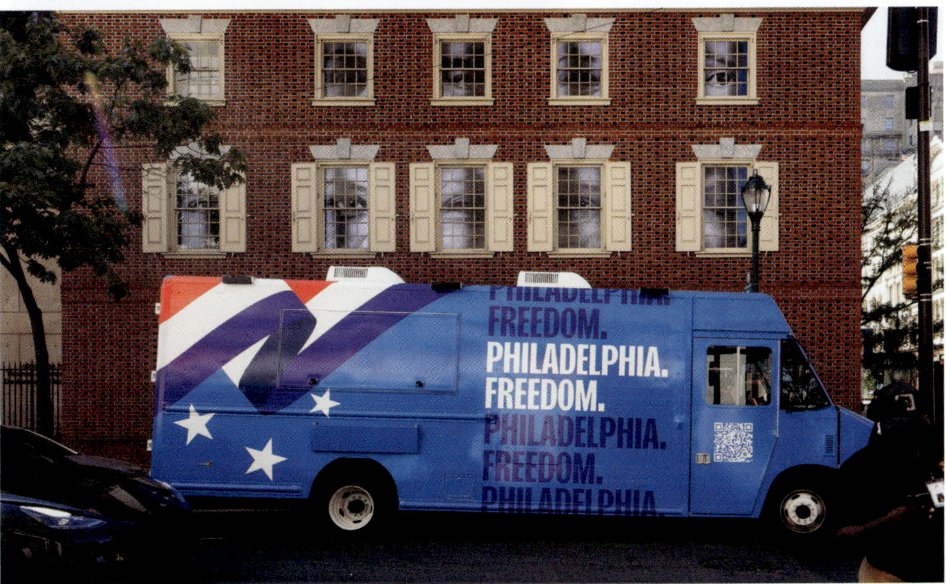

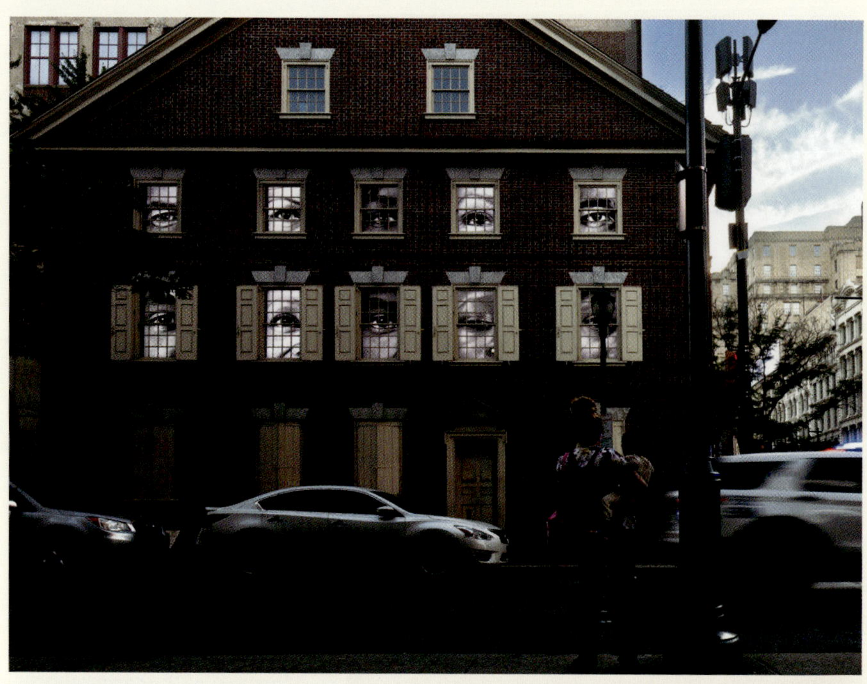

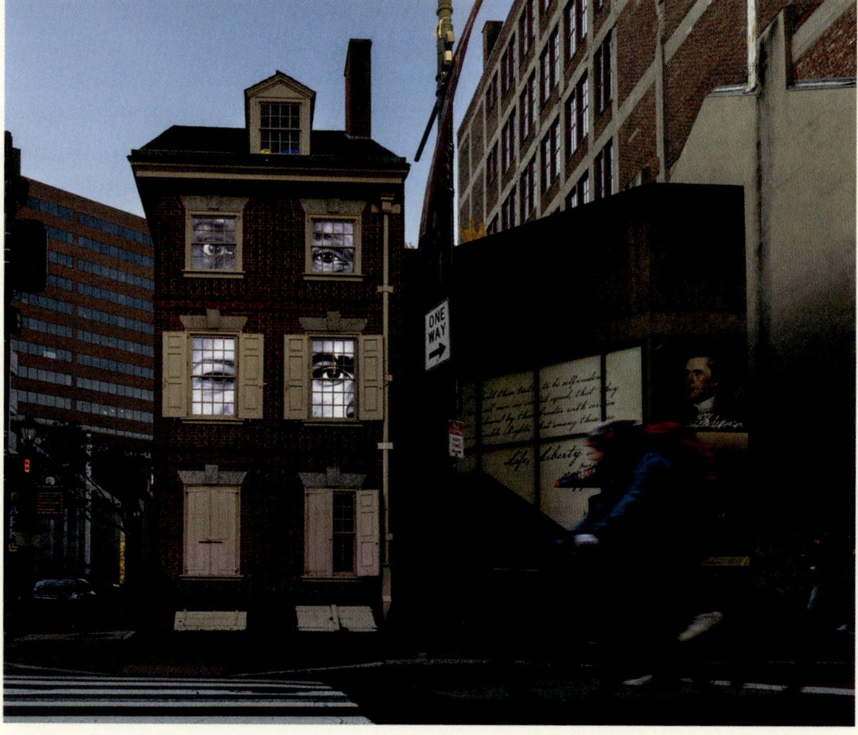
ONE
WAY

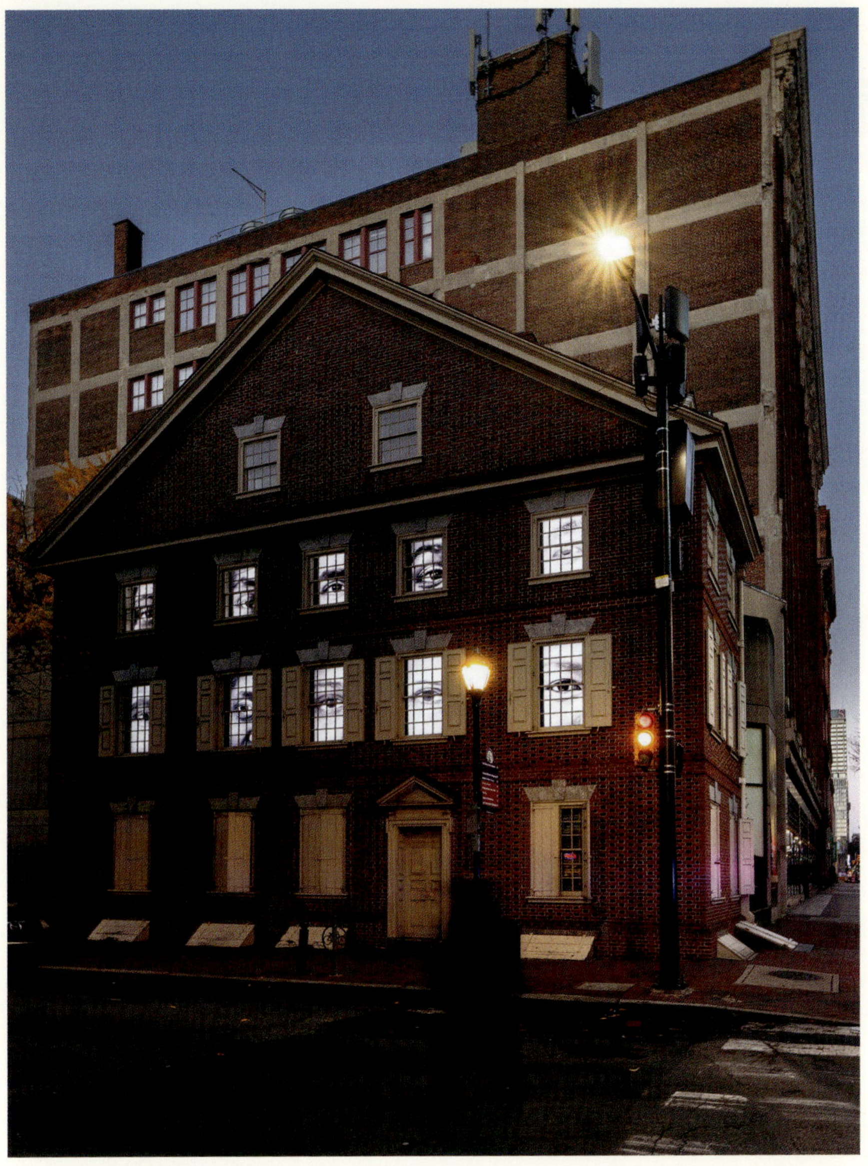

Declaration House was rebuilt in the 1970s to resemble the site where Thomas Jefferson and Robert Hemmings stayed while Jefferson drafted the Declaration of Independence. It lay abandoned for decades. Sonya Clark's "The Descendants of Monticello" brought the site back to life and situated Hemmings's legacy at the forefront of American history.

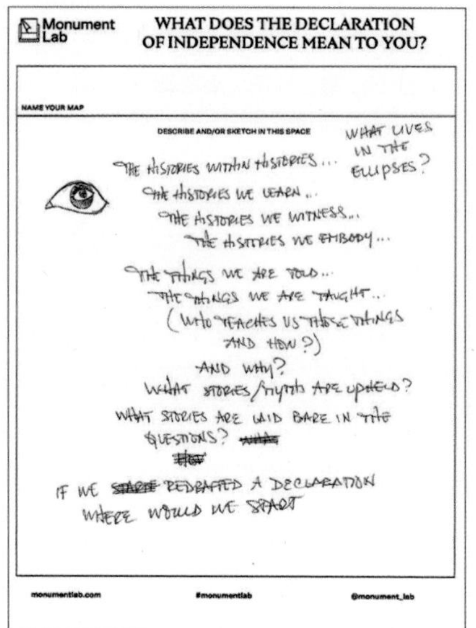
Monument Lab
WHAT DOES THE DECLARATION OF INDEPENDENCE MEAN TO YOU?

NAME YOUR MAP

DESCRIBE AND/OR SKETCH IN THIS SPACE

WHAT LIVES IN THE ELLIPSES?

THE HISTORIES WITHIN HISTORIES...
THE HISTORIES WE LEARN...
THE HISTORIES WE WITNESS...
THE HISTORIES WE EMBODY...

THE THINGS WE ARE TOLD...
THE THINGS WE ARE TAUGHT...
(WHO TEACHES US THESE THINGS AND HOW?)
AND WHY?
WHAT STORIES/MYTHS ARE UPHELD?
WHAT STORIES ARE LAID BARE IN THE QUESTIONS?

IF WE REDRAFTED A DECLARATION
WHERE WOULD WE START

monumentlab.com #monumentlab @monument_lab

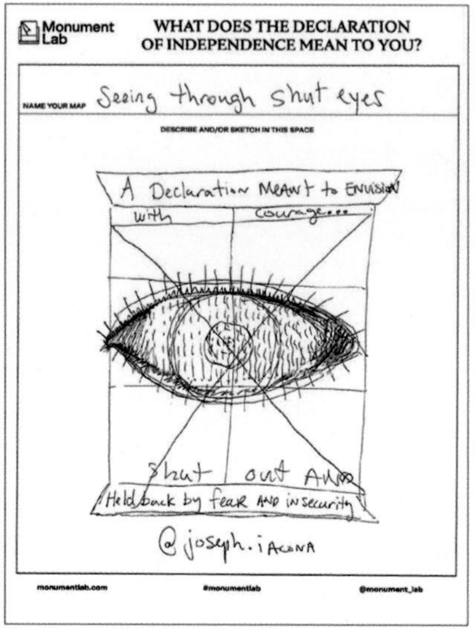
Monument Lab
WHAT DOES THE DECLARATION OF INDEPENDENCE MEAN TO YOU?

NAME YOUR MAP Seeing through shut eyes

DESCRIBE AND/OR SKETCH IN THIS SPACE

A Declaration Meant to Envision with courage...
Shut out AND
Held back by fear AND insecurity

@joseph.iacona

monumentlab.com #monumentlab @monument_lab

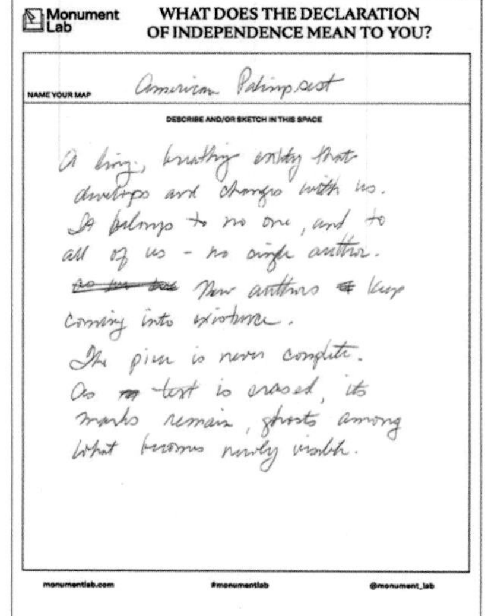
Monument Lab
WHAT DOES THE DECLARATION OF INDEPENDENCE MEAN TO YOU?

NAME YOUR MAP American Palimpsest

DESCRIBE AND/OR SKETCH IN THIS SPACE

A living, breathing entity that develops and changes with us.
It belongs to no one, and to all of us - no single author.
New authors keep coming into existence.
The piece is never complete.
As text is erased, its marks remain, ghosts among what becomes newly visible.

monumentlab.com #monumentlab @monument_lab

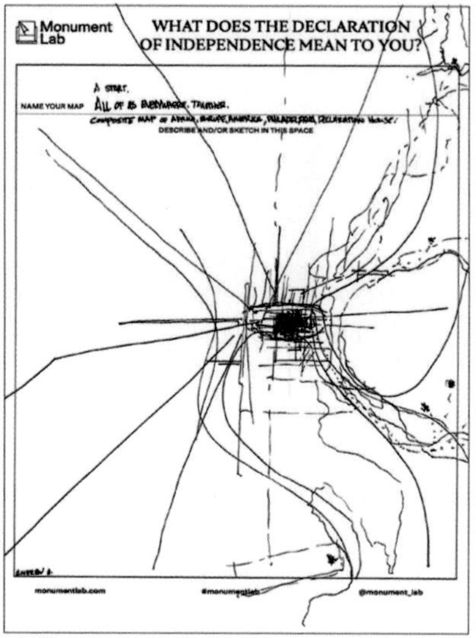
Monument Lab
WHAT DOES THE DECLARATION OF INDEPENDENCE MEAN TO YOU?

A START.
NAME YOUR MAP ALL OF US EVERYWHERE. TOGETHER.

DESCRIBE AND/OR SKETCH IN THIS SPACE

monumentlab.com #monumentlab @monument_lab

Collected public story forms from *Declaration House*.

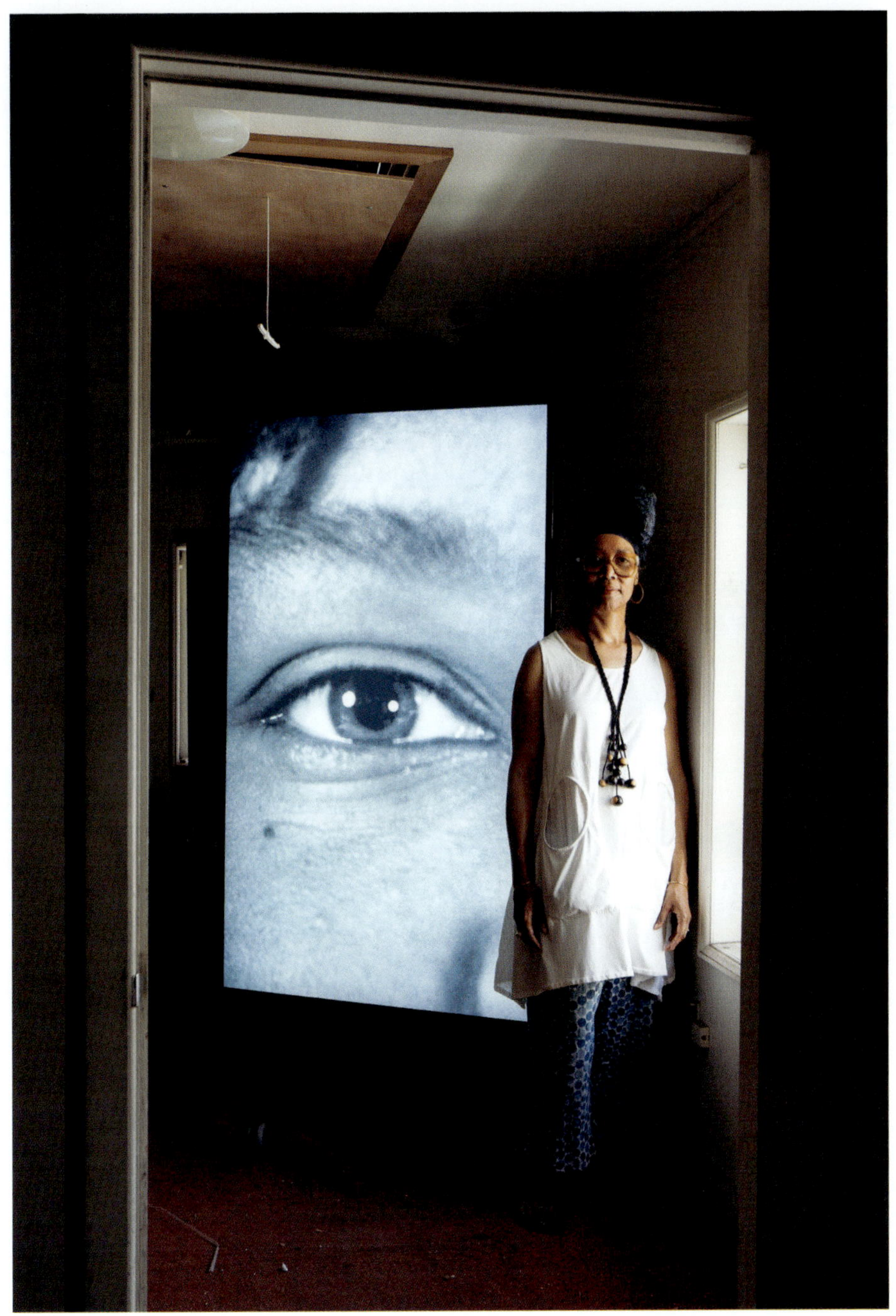

Sonya Clark site visit to Declaration House, Philadelphia, PA, 2023.

# Can I Grow a Witness?

## *Meditations on Trees as Kindred, Kindred as Trees*

Yolanda Wisher

The tree of liberty must be refreshed from time to time
with the blood of patriots and tyrants.[1]
—**Thomas Jefferson**

One upas tree overshadows us all.[2]
—**Frederick Douglass**

^ ^ ^

Before I visited Monticello, Thomas Jefferson's Virginia plantation, I read about its Mulberry Row, the ten-foot-wide, thousand-foot-long path "shaded and sheltered by an allée of fruit-producing mulberry trees,"[3] where enslaved artisans lived and labored from the 1770s to 1820s. On Monticello's Mulberry Row, Black girls and others—artistic ancestors of renowned fiber and textile artist Sonya Clark[4]—wove the fabric that clothed hundreds of people on the Monticello plantation.[5] According to historian C. Dierksheide, "Jefferson had various names for this place—'Mulberry-row' in 1782, 'Mulberry Lane' in 1793, and 'Mulberry walk' in 1808."[6] The original rows of mulberry trees at Monticello have not survived, but a new group was planted in 1995.

Although he catalogued far more trees than he planted, Jefferson was deemed "the father of American forestry," his adoration and respect for trees, like many aspects of his character, aggrandized into mythological proportions. During a dinner conversation in the President's House in Philadelphia, he once remarked, "The unnecessary felling of a tree, perhaps the growth of centuries, seems to me a crime little short of murder."[7] Jefferson drew from more than 160 species of trees, including mulberries, to shape and ornament the Monticello plantation.[8] He used these trees like ink to write upon the visual landscape of Monticello's gardens and grounds, crafting iconic alcoves of shade and vistas of light with their slow growth and patient grandeur.

While Jefferson may have masterminded the arboreal paradise of Monticello, the enslaved Black folks who lived there and at his other plantation, Poplar Forest, tended to and worked closely with the trees. These folks included John Hemmings, the brother of Robert Hemmings, a highly skilled joiner and cabinetmaker born in 1776 who "started his working life as an 'out-carpenter,' felling trees and hewing logs, building fences and barns, and helping to construct the log slave dwellings on Mulberry Row."[9] John worked closely and lovingly with wood, making wooden presents for Jefferson's grandchildren. He constructed a lap desk for Jefferson's granddaughter Ellen that was lost in a shipwreck on the way to Boston. He also crafted much of the woodwork and furniture inside the Monticello house and Poplar Forest. Jefferson was buried in a wooden coffin that is believed to have been made by Hemmings. In a letter to Jefferson dated October 20, 1819, John Hemmings reported on his work at Poplar Forest, writing intimately and in detail about his use of pine and poplar:

> dear sir . . . I am now abut the shetters i hav pine enough for stils and reals of 6 windowrs i have got them al radey to put togatehear . . . i am now giting the in sid suff reddy we hav anough poplar but have it to slit with the saw but as it is seaisond we reather have it for fear of scrinking that is all the pine plank we hav hear M^r yeancey sayes that he cand get som that is enough to do the remandour . . .[10]

Deeply acquainted with the haven of Virginia's old-growth forests, John Hemmings channeled the mutability of its trees into his creation of beloved objects of beauty and function, many of which survive to this day.

Toward the end of "Picturing Mulberry Row at Monticello," a short video on the historic estate's website, an aerial shot of archaeological excavations of the site shows the large, uncovered roots of a tree intertwined among the brick and stone foundations of living quarters on Mulberry Row.[11] This Kentucky

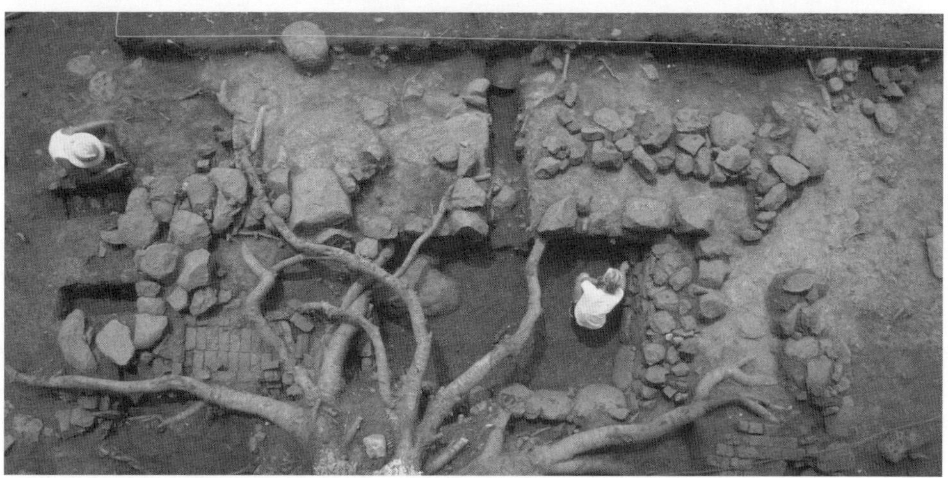

Still from "Picturing Mulberry Row at Monticello," timestamp 4:17.

coffee tree, dating to the late nineteenth century or early twentieth century,[12] perhaps tended and touched by Black hands, held watch over a community of Black people with whom its roots were interwoven.

Thinking about the trees on Mulberry Row at Monticello, I was reminded of Lucille Clifton's poem "mulberry fields."[13] In the poem, Clifton uplifts the voices and spirits of unnamed enslaved folks who have been buried in graves marked by rocks and stones carelessly disturbed and "piled into a barn" by modern stewards of a plantation on Maryland's Eastern Shore. In the absence of these "shaped" headstones "scratched with triangles and other forms," Clifton writes that "wild berries warm a field of bones," almost as if the trees had comforted the fields with their fruit. In another poem, "at the cemetery, walnut grove plantation, south carolina, 1989," Clifton again acknowledges the timeless silence created by rocks meant to mark the graves of the enslaved: "among the rocks / at walnut grove / your silence drumming / in my bones," imploring them to "tell me your names."[14] In both poems, the presence of walnut and mulberry trees marks the absence of the stories and names of enslaved people in a refusal of forgetting, a way to bookmark what has been lost.

In her book *Trace: Memory, History, Race, and the American Landscape*, geologist Lauret Savoy writes:

> The silence of Walnut Grove's burying grounds seemed to belie the enslaver's power to extract work without consent from the enslaved. Not just work, but blood, breath, life itself. Silence reminded me, too, of pieces erased from a many-storied past: complex communities excised, interior lives of "property-in-person" ignored.[15]

Clifton ends the poem "mulberry fields" by encouraging the seeds that fall on this sacred but "forsaken" ground to "bloom how you must." This final line seems to remind the ancestors and the reader that what is buried and thrown away about the legacy of slavery is never truly lost. Not only that, these seemingly adrift stories will find a way to come to the surface and into the light of day.

If the mulberry is a humble and ordinary character on the grounds of Monticello—a tree that can grow anywhere, even in soil that is wanting—the tulip poplar is its fancier, grander distant cousin, Jefferson's Juno, a member of the elegant magnolia family. During a visit to Monticello in January 2024, I saw the remains of a tulip poplar tree that Jefferson had prized as a pet in his gardens and most likely planted in the early 1800s. The original tree on the north side of the house was eventually cut down to a stump in the early 2000s because it was in danger of falling on the structure. After it was cut down, another tulip poplar, connected to the original root stock, began to grow in the middle of the stump.[16] For the group of us visiting Monticello that day, this tree sprouting a new generation from its depths, sheltered by the storied walls of the past, became a symbol of the *Declaration House* project. This grande dame of a tulip poplar stump was electric with the memory of what once was at its very core. And in its presence, we could hear something beyond/between the air around us: the ghosts of the past, insistent on being known and acknowledged.

Walking along Mulberry Row, turning in my palm some of the dirt from under the newly planted mulberry trees, I wondered about the connections and conversations that must have transpired between enslaved people and mulberry trees, and trees in general, on the grounds of Monticello. What must it have felt like for trees and humans alike to be planted far from their point of origin and forced to adapt to strange environs? What did it mean to make a new community out of a forced forest? We were there to learn more about the lives of Robert Hemmings and other enslaved Black folks on Jefferson's plantation, and the trees at Monticello were talking to us, telling us something about the Black hands and hearts of their caretakers, and the social life of Monticello, friendships and families of ancestors and descendants like a subterranean blues, vibrating with survival.

xxx

*(this writing, too, an act of weaving)*

I am a descendant of trees.

Apple trees from an orchard in Virginia annexed by the army for a fort. My ancestors were forced to abandon their orchard for elsewhere. Apple trees haunt me. My great-grandmother fed me pale morsels of apple from the blade of her paring knife, attempting to re-create memories of an apple I would never taste, that had been lost to generations. After her funeral, I climbed a young tree in our backyard in North Wales, Pennsylvania, and sat in the crook of its arm for hours, talking to the sky, hoping she might hear nine-year-old me. Trees are my chosen family. Trees have always been my telephone line to ancestors.

There were the magnificent trees at my artist residency at the Headlands Center for the Arts in Sausalito, California[17]—eucalyptus trees with limber leaves hanging and swaying like bodies. These trees, smelling so fresh and clean, are hated because they courted the fires raging across California at the end of 2024. They used to be one of many varieties of hanging trees, on which Indigenous, Black, Asian, and Latinx people were murdered. They are some of the country's youngest "witness trees," centuries-old trees that were present during a major historical or cultural event. They are also twisted "liberty trees," what Jared Farmer describes as "landmarks of the civic freedom to commit violence in support of white nationalism . . . vegetal manifestations of toxic masculinity."[18] How many trees still stand as witnesses to lynchings, like Paul Laurence Dunbar's "Haunted Oak," "burned with dread" by the memory of the horrors done upon them?

*I feel the rope against my bark,*
*And the weight of him in my grain,*
*I feel in the throe of his final woe*
*The touch of my own last pain.*[19]

I didn't expect to learn about a history of lynching trees on the West Coast, but I came across artist Ken Gonzales-Day's photographs, in which he erases the human bodies from archival lynching photographs, emphasizing and throwing into relief the body of the tree. Gonzales-Day's project of finding the source of his art through the process of looking at photos and historical documents echoes Clark's work on "The Descendants of Monticello." He writes:

> It might sound strange to say that the work did not begin as a project about lynching. It was a project about place and the people who inhabited it.... It is my hope that the *absence* inferred in this work may one day be seen as contributing to social justice movements, adding to the history of our nation....[20]

In Gonzales-Day's work, as in Clifton's poems, trees bear witness to and hold space for those people who have been relegated to the shadows of history.

*In the positive and negative space that trees occupy above and below ground, and even inside their core, they hold a powerful presence and absence that is in deep, ancient conversation with all beings on earth. The trees felt things and bear witness. They know the unnamed and home the unlocatable. They are not blind, and they can't turn away. There are trees that grow alone and don't talk to other trees. There are trees that grow around a stump like a family. Trees like to grow around other trees. Trees like to be in forests. There is an etiquette to their existence that is troubled by having to grow in private gardens, arboretums, or plantations. They don't want to be pets. They want to be free, like all of us. They want to live and let live. They want to grow old together. Tree time is like CPT*[21]*—they do things when they're ready and in their own due time. They stay put, though. They must remain on guard as long as they live. They can never escape, even after being felled or burned. The roots lie underground, waiting for renewal.*

I wonder about trees as humanity's first monuments, our first monuments to family and community bonds—y'know, the urge to do/bury/dance/sing/ dream up/under/next to/beneath a tree? In Philadelphia, we tell origin stories about trees in our street names and in our folklore, about the Treaty Elm where William Penn acquired the land for the city from the Lenape in 1683. Or we can go back before Penn got there, when the Lenape cultivated the forest with fire, shaping swaths of land like a community garden. Living in Philly, we can't always forget that we are living in what used to be a fully forested city. Much of the city's development was located up and down the Delaware River, while the westward areas were not developed. Not far from Declaration House in Washington Square Park, there used to stand Philadelphia's Moon Tree, a sycamore grown from a seed that had gone to the moon with the Apollo 14 mission but that ultimately didn't survive life in Philadelphia, in America, or on Earth. This tree was planted in honor of the country's Bicentennial in 1976, the year I was born, in a park that used to be a potter's field and a cemetery for Black people.[22] What sagacious and wily things would Octavia Butler have said about this Moon Tree trying to grow in that solemn soil and failing? I think of the early Philadelphia trees that Robert Hemmings must have encountered among the arboreal grid of city streets, on the outskirts of the city near the Declaration House on Seventh and Market where he stayed with Jefferson as he wrote the Declaration of Independence. The streets nearby were then named for trees: Cedar (now South), Pine, Spruce, Walnut, Chestnut, Mulberry (now Arch), and Sassafras (now Race).[23] These trees, like Hemmings, were observers and stewards of the revolutionary spirit churning in the city. I imagine him seeking the shade of some of these trees when waiting for Jefferson or running his errands in the summer of 1776, when temperatures could be "in the upper 80s or low 90s."[24] Or avoiding the whipping post, possibly made from an oak tree, at Second and Market. Maybe encountering the work of enslaved Africans who felled wood to make room for farm lands[25] reminded him of his brother John back in Virginia. Perhaps he visited Southeast Square,[26] also known as Congo Square, only a few minutes' walk from the site of the Declaration House. Congo Square in Philadelphia was a place where free and enslaved folks gathered to find joy through song and dance, and to bury their dead.[27] Hemmings would have seen it years before it was converted from pasture to park with plantings of Lombardy poplars in 1794.[28] Like its counterpart in New Orleans, where the magnificent

Eggun Tree or Ancestor Tree, a live oak, held center stage, Congo Square in Philadelphia, even without many trees, was a sacred space to commune with ancestors and spirits.

*Trees are the souls of men,*
*Reaching skyward*
*And while each soul*
*Draws nearer God*
*Its dark roots cleave*
*To earthly sod. . . .*[29]

At Monticello, as we visited the graves of enslaved folks, Clark told us about how scholar and writer Imani Perry was writing about periwinkle in the forest as a sign—a haunting—of Black burials.[30] Without mortar and stone, they made monuments of what they could grow with their own hands; they made an understory. Monument Lab fellow, artist, activist, writer, and architectural researcher Imani Jacqueline Brown researches and writes about groves of magnolia trees in her home state of Louisiana that have sprung up to mark and remember the burial of enslaved ancestors. In "black ecologies: an opening, an offering," she writes, "Black ecologies wink into existence as resistance to plantation ecologies. Ecological resistance emerges from the cypress trees in whose crowns we crouch, muskets over shoulders, listening for dogs. . . ."[31] In other words, the cypress trees have done more than remember; they have guarded and had our backs.

+ + +

*the forest a free jazz.*
*the body of a tree, free jazz.*
*improvisation all over*
*the place.*

The giant redwoods of Muir Woods, something to see on my bucket list, were finally checked off during my travels in California. As I walked through the giant cathedral of trees with my residency housemate Hanna Tuulikki, she talked about the enchanted forests in her mother's home of Finland and the ways that folks there regard the forest, an army or neighborhood of trees, with awe and terror. That day, in one of the oldest forests in North America, we trespassed into the bowels of trees and tasted wild clover at their trunk-feet.

I came home to Philadelphia still looking for meaning in trees and my life with trees as a Black woman, someone who has spent most of her life in the suburbs and city. Wondering, as I often do, about how to reclaim the apple orchards annexed by the army. How to reclaim that talking grandmother of a tree in my backyard, now disappeared by a fence a neighbor put up without asking. Or the tree out front that the potter who once lived in my house planted to make a Japanese garden here in my Germantown neighborhood of Philadelphia, about eight miles northwest of Declaration House; a little like Jefferson, she sought to create a paradise where there used to be old forest. No one can tell us what kind of tree it is; one of the older neighbors once said it was an overgrown shrub.

And how to decode the mystery of Maple Street, the place where our family home in Ambler, Pennsylvania, used to exist. Or the crimson-red *Acer palmatum* in my mother's backyard, the one with the long arm that could not withstand our swinging or lounging upon with a good book. Or the green Japanese maple baby that my love, Mark, brought home from Shofuso,[32] which I planted while six months pregnant and is now a strong and sturdy fifteen-year-old like my son, Thelonious. Or the gloriously thick silver maple tree in our backyard that heaved down its final heavy limb across the patio, just minutes after my dad had asked for my forgiveness for being absent for three decades of my life and we had walked back into the house more family than we'd ever been. This life with trees is no joke. The relationship between humans and trees is elemental—and for Black folks, essential—to remember and reclaim. Like the tree-shaped scar of slavery's brutality upon Sethe's back in Toni Morrison's novel *Beloved* or the pear tree of Janie's life and sexual awakening in Zora Neale Hurston's *Their Eyes Were Watching God*, trees embody Black memory and magic and an unbreakable bond across centuries of struggle.

- - -

There's a reason why we call them "family trees." Sitting around a table at Monticello, flipping through scrapbooks of Polaroids with the team of the Getting Word African American History Department, I thought of Etheridge

Knight's poem "The Idea of Ancestry." In the poem, he ponders the "47 black faces" in photographs of family members taped to the "gray stone wall" of his jail cell. The photographs arranged on the wall become a visual family tree that Etheridge can reflect and meditate upon. They are evidence of family bonds, activated and renewed by the "falling leaves" of autumn outside the jail that "stir [his] genes," a cue and a symbol of family connections that are broken through change and circumstance, seasons of survival.[33]

Growing up without my birth father, not meeting him until my wedding day at age thirty, I have been a blank space in the family tree. This painful sense of my own blank space in our history has made me the family genealogist, looking for ancestors like my life depended on it. Trying to make sense of the missing, the unknown. And I think about the apple-tree ancestors too. The ones that were talking to us before we had to leave and go north, like samaras or winged fruits, maple keys alighting, spinning into new directions, carrying the seeds of our futures. The original trees we tended down south, missing our touch.

As we walked through the church of trees at Muir Woods, Hanna kept saying there's so much we can learn from trees. One of the first things we saw when entering the forest was a squadron of younger trees surrounding an older, burned-out stump, similar to the tulip-poplar shell at Monticello. The signage in front of this grouping is titled "Family Circles" and reads:

> Hundreds of years ago a single large redwood grew here. Then disaster struck. The trunk of the large redwood was killed, perhaps by repeated and severe wildfire. . . . Despite such terrible damage, the tree did not die. Below the ground, its massive root system was full of vitality. Before long, hundreds of young, bright green burl sprouts began to come up around the circle formed by the root crown of the original tree.[34]

Reading and witnessing this display of intergenerational care, I recalled that like us, trees know how to make families out of distance and disaster, out of love lost. We have always been listening to and mimicking the trees. As my friend and colleague Kerry Bickford has said, "The relationship extends beyond roots, too, to the many ways seeds have evolved to move and take flight. Fruit evolved so that our bodies would consume and carry seeds. Symbiosis so foundational we often forget."

> *I know now we are a family of maple trees. The color of whiskey, the color of charcoal, the color of asbestos ash. A long line of trees stretching back through time. A slow drag across Earth, against death. We breathe the tall air, sometimes luscious, sometimes laced. And you can try to kill us, but living is just what we do. Life is a family heirloom, a grove of silver maples, endangered and unprotected, our sad-sweet sap an acquired taste. Like a row of mulberries, we can grow anywhere—Norway, Brazil, Los Angeles, Virginia, Ambler. Sometimes we stay where we're planted, tending to the older trees, the baby cousins. We are medicine and balm for the world, the squirrel, the moth and woodpecker, the deer.*

Yes, the trees are like us and more than us. We can see our faces in their bark, the phenomenon of pareidolia (a form of haunting). They have eyes called burls. A tree's burl stores the same genetic material as the tree itself. It's a way for a tree to clone itself. For coastal redwoods in their forest setting, burls are the buds of new trees sprouting from the fallen or felled. New roots and buds are signs of regeneration. It's worth mentioning here Clark's work with the symbolism of trees in her own practice in 2002, including *mitosis*,[35] with branches of copper reaching across the work seeking a kinship with one another, and *roots and branches*,[36] which illustrates a familial resemblance between a branch made out of copper and another made out of human hair. In *two trees*,[37] two branches woven out of black thread grow straight from a scalp, evoking the patterns of regrowth in Muir Woods and Monticello.[38] Similarly, the eyes of "The Descendants of Monticello," descendants of Robert Hemmings, their roots entangled with Jefferson's, are burls on the tree of this country; they are monuments as earthly and otherworldly as a tree becoming itself. If ancestors live in our souls and in our eyes, as Clark insists, not just in our music or poems but in our very essence, then the eyes of "The Descendants of Monticello" are the soul of a young Black man peering into a two-faced America.

The *Declaration House* project and Clark's "The Descendants of Monticello" move us toward a definition of monument that is embodied as sentinel, as witness, as treetop, as burl—an old-new tree that watches over us, whose fruits feed us, that holds our freedoms and unfreedoms.[39]

Haitian revolutionary Toussaint Louverture,[40] born thirty-five years after Hemmings and three years after Hemmings was freed by Jefferson, famously said, "In overthrowing me, you have overthrown only the trunk of the tree of liberty; but the roots remain; they will push out again, because they are numerous, and go deep into the soil."[41] *Declaration House* is an outgrowth of the many daily rebellions that allowed Hemmings's spirit to carry on through his descendants as well as the effort and impulse of many generations of Black folks, a pushing out, a reaching skyward, a going deep for a freedom not promised, but inherent.

## NOTES

1. In a letter dated November 13, 1787, from Thomas Jefferson to William Stephens Smith, the son-in-law of John Adams.

2. Frederick Douglass, *Life and Times of Frederick Douglass Written by Himself* (Cleveland: George M. Rewell, 1883). The upas tree is in the mulberry family and contains a poisonous latex.

3. Gardiner Hallock, "Mulberry Row: Telling the Story of Slavery at Monticello," *Site-LINES: A Journal of Place* 14, no. 2 (Spring 2019): 4, https://www.jstor.org/stable/26608851.

4. Two of Clark's earlier artworks, *two trees* (hat), 2003, and *Rooted and Uprooted*, 2011, show the artist's preoccupation with trees, like hair, as conduits of Black ancestry.

5. Karen Hampton, "African American Women: Plantation Textile Production from 1750 to 1830," in *Approaching Textiles, Varying Viewpoints: Proceedings of the Seventh Biennial Symposium of the Textile Society of America, Santa Fe, New Mexico, 2000*, 266–267, https://digitalcommons.unl.edu/tsaconf/770.

6. C. Dierksheide, "What Was Mulberry Row?," *Monticello Blog*, May 5, 2011, https://monticello-www.s3.us-east-1.amazonaws.com/files/pdfs/archived-pages/blog/2011-05-05_what-was-mulberry-row.pdf.

7. Thomas Jefferson Foundation, "Trees at Monticello," *Thomas Jefferson Encyclopedia*, https://www.monticello.org/house-gardens/farms-gardens/landscape-features/trees-at-monticello/.

8. Thomas Jefferson Foundation, "Trees at Monticello."

9. Thomas Jefferson Foundation, "John Hemmings," *Thomas Jefferson Encyclopedia*, https://www.monticello.org/research-education/thomas-jefferson-encyclopedia/john-hemmings/.

10. John Hemmings, "John Hemmings to Thomas Jefferson, 20 October 1819," Founders Online, https://founders.archives.gov/?q=Correspondent%3A%22Hemmings%2C%20John%20%28Hemings%29%22%20Correspondent%3A%22Jefferson%2C%20Thomas%22&s=1111311111&r=2.

11. Thomas Jefferson's Monticello, "Picturing Mulberry Row at Monticello," YouTube, March 9, 2020, https://youtu.be/xoKwrN2kPIg?si=KJ3PiccbpMiBXqHS.

12. Fraser D. Neiman, the director of archaeology at Monticello, writes, "The site in the photo, from the early 1980s, is the 'Building o Site,' named after the structure that stood there

in 1796 when Thomas Jefferson drew a plat of Mulberry Row to accompany an insurance policy. The photo shows two foundation fragments, probably for two different houses, based on their slightly different alignments. . . . We know that George Rogers Clark sent Jefferson seeds of his tree in the 1780's. The tree died several decades ago and its remains have been removed. But the stump is still visible!"

13. Lucille Clifton, "mulberry fields," in *Mercy: Poems* (Rochester, NY: BOA Editions, 2004). I first encountered and studied this poem at the Furious Flower teacher seminar on Clifton's work led by Hilary Holladay in 2009 at James Madison University in Harrisonburg, Virginia.

14. Lucille Clifton, "at the cemetery, walnut grove plantation, south carolina, 1989," in *The Collected Poems of Lucille Clifton 1965–2010*, eds. Kevin Young and Michael S. Glaser (Rochester, NY: BOA Editions, 2012).

15. Lauret Savoy, *Trace: Memory, History, Race, and the American Landscape* (Berkeley: Counterpoint Press, 2015), 111.

16. Thomas Jefferson's Monticello, "Monticello's Tulip Poplars," YouTube, November 26, 2021, https://www.youtube.com/watch?v=cZncGSwJHUk.

17. I was in residence there in October 2024.

18. Jared Farmer, "In America, Trees Symbolize Both Freedom and Unfreedom," *OUPblog*, April 26, 2019, https://blog.oup.com/2019/04/america-trees-freedom/#:~:text=Early%20members%20of%20the%20Republican%20Party%20spoke,unfreedom%20only%20occasionally%20appeared%20in%20nineteenth%2Dcentury%20media.

19. Paul Laurence Dunbar, "The Haunted Oak," in *The Complete Poems of Paul Laurence Dunbar* (New York: Dodd, Mead, 1913).

20. Ken Gonzales-Day, "Searching for California Hang Trees," in *Survey Practices and Landscape Photography across the Globe*, eds. Sophie Junge and Erin Hyde Nolan (New York: Routledge, 2023); excerpt available at https://kengonzalesday.com/projects/hang-trees/.

21. Colored People's Time. As Rasheedah Phillips describes, "On most plantations, 'the masters ha[d] complete control over the distribution of the negro's time.' (Slavery Meeting at Colchester, Essex County Standard, January 19, 1838). As Black people sought more control over their own time and labor after the Civil War, the tropes would later morph into 'negro time' and an evolution of the phrase 'colored people's time,' co-associating Black time and Black people with lateness and laziness." See Rasheedah Phillips, "Colonized Time, Racial Time, and the Legal Time of Progress," *Poverty and Race* 31, no. 1 (Jan–Sept 2022), https://www.prrac.org/pdf/Jan-Sept2022.pdf.

22. Bradley Crowe, "Philadelphia's Moon Tree," *Atlas Obscura*, October 11, 2016, https://www.atlasobscura.com/places/philadelphias-moon-tree.

23. Laura Turner Igoe, "Trees," *The Encyclopedia of Greater Philadelphia*, November 22, 2013, https://philadelphiaencyclopedia.org/essays/trees-2/.

24. Cherri Gregg, "How Philadelphians Handled Heatwaves in 1776," CBS News, June 20, 2012, https://www.cbsnews.com/philadelphia/news/how-philadelphians-handled-heatwaves-in-1776/.

25. Michael D'Onofrio, "Slavery and Philly: Since Arrival of First Enslaved Africans, Deep Scars Exists [*sic*] Here, across Commonwealth," WHYY, August 20, 2019, https://whyy.org/articles/slavery-and-philly-since-arrival-of-first-enslaved-africans-deep-scars-exists-here-across-commonwealth/.

26. Now known as Washington Square, one of the five original city squares that William Penn envisioned to make Philadelphia a "greene Countrie Towne."

27. John Kopp, "Washington Square: From Mass Graves to Mass Media," *PhillyVoice*, April 10, 2017, https://www.phillyvoice.com/washington-square-mass-graves-mass-media/.

28. "History of Early American Landscape Design: Washington Square (Philadelphia, PA)," National Gallery of Art, revised August 30, 2021, https://heald.nga.gov/mediawiki/index.php/Washington_Square_(Philadelphia,_PA).

29. Edward Silvera, "Finality," *FIRE!! A Quarterly Devoted to the Younger Negro Artists* 1, no. 1 (November 1926).

30. Imani Perry, *Black in Blues: How a Color Tells the Story of My People* (New York: Ecco, 2025), 53.

31. Imani Jacqueline Brown, "Black Ecologies: An opening, an offering," Imani Jacqueline Brown Official Website, https://imanijacquelinebrown.net/Black-Ecologies-an-opening-an-offering.

32. The Japanese House and Garden in Philadelphia.

33. Etheridge Knight, "The Idea of Ancestry," in *The Essential Etheridge Knight* (Pittsburgh: University of Pittsburgh Press, 1986), 12–13.

34. Signage from Muir Woods National Monument in California, November 2024.

35. Sonya Clark, *mitosis*, Sonya Clark Official Website, 2002, http://sonyaclark.com/gallery/mitosis/.

36. Sonya Clark, *roots and branches*, Sonya Clark Official Website, 2002, http://sonyaclark.com/gallery/roots-and-branches/.

37. Sonya Clark, *two trees*, Sonya Clark Official Website, 2002, http://sonyaclark.com/gallery/two-trees/.

38. I am indebted to Kerry Bickford for illuminating these connections for me.

39. Farmer, "In America."

40. While Jefferson was president, the United States cancelled aid to Louverture in fear that the Haitian revolution would spread to this country, and he refused to recognize Haitian independence. The United States did not recognize Haiti's status as a sovereign, independent nation until 1862. "The United States and the Haitian Revolution, 1791–1804," U.S. Department of State Archive, https://2001-2009.state.gov/r/pa/ho/time/nr/91724.htm#:~:text=Under%20President%20Thomas%20Jefferson's%20presidency,as%20a%20sovereign%2C%20independent%20nation.

41. Farmer, "In America."

# Family Monuments

Niya Bates

"Do you think it'll be scary?," Granger Pascall asked while opening his eyes as wide as he could, encircling his little fingers around them like a magnifying glass. His feet dangled over the edge of a bench in the hallway of Kenwood House, where the Getting Word African American History Department at Monticello (Getting Word) offices were located. Granger waited with his grandmother, Jacqueline Estes, to have his photograph taken by artist Sonya Clark and photographers from Monument Lab for the *Declaration House* exhibition. They had come to their portrait appointment on that February afternoon with a cousin, Deborah Granger, and together, over lunch, excitedly dreamed about the final form of the future art installation. A descendant of Isaac Granger, who was born enslaved at Thomas Jefferson's Monticello plantation in 1775, Granger, not yet school-age, was the youngest participant in the *Declaration House* project.

George Granger Sr., Ursula Granger, and their sons George Jr. and Bagwell were the first members of their family to come to Monticello. They arrived in 1773, just before the Hemings family, after Jefferson purchased most of the Grangers from his wife's former brother-in-law and bought the elder George Granger from another slaveholder.[1] The Grangers had their fourth son, Isaac, just a couple of years later (a third, Archy Granger, died in infancy in 1774), and by then they held important positions within the enslaved community on the Monticello mountaintop. George Sr. cared for Jefferson's orchards before being promoted to overseer, and Ursula was the head cook, a laundress, a cider brewer, and a wet nurse.[2] Isaac eventually learned the blacksmithing trade from his older brother George Jr. There is no question that they would have known Robert Hemmings, the enslaved teen who accompanied[3] Jefferson to Philadelphia in 1775 and 1776 when he drafted the Declaration of Independence. So, it was a full-circle moment for the Granger descendants to be among the participants in the *Declaration House* exhibition that sought to honor Hemmings's presence in Philadelphia.

The Getting Word team is unaware of any living descendants of Hemmings, but many of the Monticello families intermarried and lived in proximity to each other for generations in an interconnected web of social and geographic ties. In February 2024, the Getting Word team invited descendants of the Grangers, Hugheses, Hubbards, Evanses, Gillettes, and other families who would have been in community with or distant relatives of Hemmings to sit for portraits that would be used for the *Declaration House* installation. In addition to living descendants, artist Sonya Clark animated historic photographs of descendants from previous generations that are preserved in the Getting Word archives at Monticello. Through the projection of a video loop of their eyes blinking from the windows of Declaration House, located at the intersection of Market and South Seventh Streets in Philadelphia, the descendants kept watch and bore witness.

Descendants' ancestries reveal just how interconnected enslaved families at Monticello were and continued to be in the century and a half after their enslavement and separation at Monticello. Photo sessions for *Declaration House* were split over two days, but each day presented opportunities for mini family reunions. On the same day that the Grangers had their portraits taken, J. Calvin Jefferson Sr., Jessica Harris, and I also had our portraits done. Our gathering reunited a community of people who would have been together at Martha Jefferson and Thomas Mann Randolph's Edgehill Plantation after the Monticello community was dispersed following Thomas Jefferson's death in 1826.[4] J. Calvin Jefferson Sr. was photographed along with his adult grandchildren, Jabari and Jade Jefferson. They descend from Robert Hughes and several other Monticello families, including the Grangers, Evanses, and Hemingses. Jessica Harris and her father, Carter Harris, are descendants of Robert Hughes's sister, Louisa. My third great-grandmother, Araminta Flemming, was enslaved at the Edgehill Plantation alongside members of the Granger and Hughes families[5] whom the Randolphs purchased after Jefferson's death. Our stories are emblematic of those of other enslaved communities in central Virginia; most Black families descended from people enslaved on central Virginia plantations ended up intermarrying at some point because many of our direct ancestors stayed in the area instead of moving north during the migrations of the twentieth century.

Reflecting on the day, Jessica Harris said, "It was powerful for us to have this shared experience . . . as people who never left. . . . Our family stayed after emancipation and built a life in the Albemarle area."[6] She added that sitting for portraits for *Declaration House* gave her and her father an opportunity to have intentional and embodied connections with their ancestors through their eyes. To participate in the process of publicly centering the history and legacy of Hemmings was rewarding and historically important work for J. Calvin Jefferson Sr. too. He has been contributing his skills as a retired archivist from the National Archives in Washington, D.C., to help Getting Word preserve its growing collections for the future. But, to participate with the next generation of his family, and to ensure that they, too, would carry the histories of their vast ancestry forward, were even more impactful for him. He plans to hang their portrait in the home he purchased in Central Virginia so that his family could be closer to his ancestral roots. He said his home is a place to gather with the family he already knew and to reconnect with the new cousins he has met through Getting Word, a place for the generations-late restoration of family ties severed by slavery.

Months later, as we stood in the July heat on the corner of Seventh and Market Streets in Philadelphia, observing past and present family members' eyes slowly blinking through each loop of the video's cycle, I recalled Granger's question and remarked out loud, "It's not scary at all!" "How could it be?," responded Clark from behind me. *Declaration House* collapsed the space between then and now and put descendants and their ancestors—free and enslaved—on the same monumental plane. Standing there, I reflected on my own family's ancestral and land-based connections to Monticello and the ways that even all these years later, so many of us have remained within the orbit of those same plantations, bound to the land, our lives intertwined. Jacqueline Estes lived in my neighborhood and was a second mom to me, but I only learned of her ties to Monticello after I started working as the director of Getting Word in 2016, which was before I learned of my own family's connection to Edgehill a handful of years later. Standing on that street corner, I found her eye, then Granger's, then mine.

Looking up at the installation, I saw generations of men, women, and children who made a way forward where there wasn't one.[7] I saw our enslaved ancestors and the communities they built and rebuilt amid constant upheaval and pruning, growth and regrowth, separations and sometimes reunions. Through the animated photos from the archive, I felt connected to those members of Getting Word whom I did not get to meet in this lifetime, but whose stories have been kept alive through oral histories and the babbling sounds of children playing on the west lawn at Monticello when we gather for events and programs. After a few minutes of reflection on that street corner at golden hour, just before sunset, the sounds I heard in the city of Philadelphia gave way to awe at what this installation had accomplished. Clark, taking in the scene herself and observing our reactions, broke through the quiet chatter among us to proclaim, "Each of us is a monument in our family tree."

Each time a descendant returns to the landscapes and sites built, traversed, and inhabited by our ancestors, a new monument is created. We each contribute new information to the archives. Each of us is composed of the genetic puzzle pieces of our ancestors. If you count back ten generations—about the number of generations between Granger and his ancestors at Monticello—it has taken 1,024 people to get each of us here. Our experiences while making *Declaration House* show the power of doing the work to connect our family trees so that future generations have a greater awareness of from whom and where they descend.

*Declaration House* spoke to the community that Hemmings lived within and knew well, and it represented the tremendous legacies left behind by the generation of unsung American founders who have been denied the same presence in documentary archives. Our presence in historic spaces like Declaration House is an act of reclamation. Our ancestors lived so we could be free.

## NOTES

1. Lucia C. Stanton, *"Those Who Labor for My Happiness": Slavery at Thomas Jefferson's Monticello* (Charlottesville: University of Virginia Press, 2012), 118–119; Andrew M. Davenport, "We Were Scattered: The African American Diaspora from Monticello, 1826–1900" (Ph.D. diss., Georgetown University, 2024), 12, 14.

2. Stanton, 119–123.

3. There are two ways to spell the Hemings/Hemmings surname. Thomas Jefferson spelled it with one *m* in his letters and daily *Farm Book*, but in surviving documents from members of the family, they spelled it with two. Getting Word uses *Hemings* when describing the family as a whole and *Hemmings* when writing about individuals within the family for whom documentary evidence shows that they spelled it that way.

4. Stanton, *"Those Who Labor for My Happiness,"* 127, 207–209.

5. Stanton, 105–211.

6. Jessica Harris, to the author on February 20, 2025.

7. Dianne Swann-Wright, *A Way Out of No Way: Claiming Family and Freedom in the New South* (Charlottesville: University of Virginia Press, 2002).

# Careful Looking

## *Tending to Images of Descendants and Ancestors*

Kerry C. Bickford

What does it mean to address irreparable wrongs through artistic work? As a project manager and producer of *Declaration House*, responsible for concretizing an idea into form, I weighed this question for months. Curators foster and safeguard the core ideas and ethics of a project, but it is frequently a producer who is on the front lines of actioning those principles. Over those months, I learned, unlearned, and relearned how to care for Robert Hemmings—his life, his memory, and his legacy.

When I joined the team that would create *Declaration House*, Sonya Clark had already proposed the concept for the artwork. In response to Declaration House, the National Park Service's 1975 reconstruction of the site where Thomas Jefferson and Robert Hemmings stayed during the Second Continental Congress, Clark would resurrect Hemmings's presence visually, "through the eyes of his descendants." Our introduction to these descendants was through Gayle Jessup White, the public relations and community engagement officer at the Thomas Jefferson Foundation and herself a descendant of the Hemings, Hubbard, and Jefferson families; and Andrew Davenport, the then-director of the Getting Word African American History Department. In our first meeting, Davenport agreed to take our proposal to a committee of descendants to review, but he also issued a caution to guide our work: By presenting this history in Philadelphia, we would be taking Hemmings out of his full context. As Annette Gordon-Reed puts forth in *The Hemingses of Monticello*, "Enslaved people's closest human associations and familiar surroundings often brought a form of stability and comfort. That was virtually all they had."[1] Hemmings's place of birth, his family, and his communities were all in Virginia. Hemmings married and raised children in Virginia; after he secured his freedom from Jefferson, Virginia was the home he chose. In highlighting his time spent in Philadelphia, we were contextualizing him squarely in his bondage.

With this caveat in mind, I traveled to Monticello as part of the project team to gather eyes for the exhibition. We spent days in the Getting Word archives, looking through photographs of Hemmings's extended family of descendants, the earliest dating back to the Civil War. In flat files and Google Drive, we sorted through studio portraits, graduation photos, shots of crowds gathered at family reunions, and images of descendants posing in front of Monticello itself. As we did, I was haunted by a line from Ross Gay's poem *Be Holding*, an adaptation of which I had seen project cocurator Yolanda Wisher perform months earlier.[2] In the poem, a reflection on joy, imaged violence, consent, and the wondrous talent of basketball great Dr. J, Gay describes a photograph of a Black woman and her young grandson taken by Farm Security Administration photographer Jack Delano.[3] Gay characterizes the posture of the boy as he leans against a doorjamb and eyes Delano:

*for he too knows*
*he's being looked at,*

*he knows*
*he's being shot,*

*he's being shared,*
*by someone who doesn't love him,*

*and so does not give his whole body*
*to the camera . . .*[4]

The photos entrusted to us by the Getting Word team ranged in centuries and settings, but they shared an intimacy of gaze and expression, a fullness of trust, the complete opposite of Gay's description of the boy in the doorjamb. I found myself tending to photographs and digitized images of bespectacled elders and ancestors, aunties in pearls and silk scarves, treasured lost grand-babies. Siblings laughed and leaned on each other; grandfathers balanced toddlers on shoulder and knee.

I had full faith that the Getting Word team had shared only photographs that were appropriate to use and that the descendants who had participated in video portrait sessions with Clark had enthusiastically consented, even traveled, to be involved in the installation. The source of my unease was an ever-deepening understanding of the responsibility that came with presenting this history. Descendant families had already given of themselves to ensure that the legacies of their ancestors could not be effaced. Now, we were taking tender images, beloveds beheld by beloveds, even further out of their contexts to share on a city block with a public that did not know them, let alone love them.

Declaration House was not an easy site to make hospitable, let alone a space to welcome photographs so full of life. The house we were working in was a 1975 re-creation of the 1776 structure, built for the American Bicentennial, and it had been closed to the public for years. Among ourselves—the curators and the producing team—we frequently called the house "haunted." Paint peeled off interior walls in sheets beneath water stains, and blinds dangled in tangles from the window frames. All heating, cooling, and running water were long defunct, and electrical breakers in the house were shut off as part of standard operating practice. With no lights behind the windows, the house's facade was dominated by rows of dark cavities between shutters.

With all these reservations and collected doubts, I had forgotten to do the most important things: Trust the artist, trust the partners, and trust the site. As a producer of public art, I'm frequently humbled by the agency of the spaces in which I work: I've seen paintings peel away from ceilings, floors refuse to hold sculpture level, grass that never regrows once a foundation is laid. Sites will bless you with a sonorous grate or a gap beneath the door. This site held an enslaved child, taken from his family for months. The sin is so great that even replaced bricks remember, and they were prepared to repent. As we loaded ever-brighter and larger screens into the period rooms, the breakers remained reliable and resolute. The eyes shone through the haze of streetlights and digital billboards; Clark compared the installation's glow to that of a lighthouse. Our team of video editors used the filmed portraits taken of living descendants as templates from which to animate the archival photographs so that they blinked and darted. Their intimacy was heightened and made active—they felt not like subjects awaiting public spectators but like protagonists.

In rebuilding Declaration House, the National Park Service had resurrected Hemmings's memory and name in the position Davenport cautioned us against—away from his community and home of choice—only to shutter the museum and summarily abandon him. Rather than preparing to share the photographs from Getting Word with a Philadelphia public, we were first and foremost gathering Hemmings's kin around him, filling the place of isolation with his context. Those trustful, beheld gazes in the archival photographs were looking straight at Robert. When Jefferson brought Hemmings to Philadelphia at fourteen years old, *he* was separating Hemmings from his family, his home, the closest things the boy had to stability and comfort. This artwork, by contrast, was an act of psychic reunification: Whatever memory, ghost, or trace of Hemmings was left at the Declaration House site, he would no longer be alone.

As citizens of the present, we can never fully redress what Jefferson and the laws of our nation stole from Hemmings. What we *can* do is tend to his legacy, care for it, by following the lead of those who love him. There was a space in Declaration House we could not safely access, in all the months we worked there—the house's top floor, with dormer windows facing north and south. In the original house, this space might have been where Hemmings slept at the end of each day of servitude: in the garret, a storage room accessible through a trapdoor, beneath the sloping roof.[5] I felt that boundary, from within the building and without. It speaks to me of everything I still don't know about the wounds of history that art and family can and cannot heal. These are generational questions. May we all take care when seeking their answers.

## NOTES

1. Annette Gordon-Reed, *The Hemingses of Monticello: An American Family* (New York: Norton, 2008), 400.

2. *Be Holding*, script by Ross Gay, composed by Tyshawn Sorey, directed by Brooke O'Harra, performed by David Gaines, Yolanda Wisher, and Yarn/Wire, Girard College, Philadelphia, May 31–June 3, 2023.

3. "This Negro woman lives with her husband and two grandchildren in an old converted schoolhouse. All the rest of her children have left the county. Heard County, Georgia." Photo by Jack Delano, Library of Congress Prints and Photographs Division, Washington, D.C.

4. Ross Gay, *Be Holding: A Poem* (Pittsburgh: University of Pittsburgh Press, 2020), 67.

5. Doris Devine Fanelli, "Furnishings Plan for Graff House, Philadelphia, PA" (Independence National Historical Park, 1988), 13, https://irma.nps.gov/DataStore/DownloadFile/603989.

# Wanted, a Genteel Servant

*for Robert Hemmings*

Paul Buchanan

that's what
he called you, brother.
you stood so dutifully as
he dressed. did
his buttons catch on
your calluses, your open-
mouthed hands? I know
he named you pet. wrote of smell,
bile, said we loved different,
*more an eager desire, than a tender*
*delicate mixture*
*of sentiment and sensation.*[1] said
we were reckless,
animals. his extensive
study in our grief
yielded the only result:
our sorrow lifts into
the air like sweat. invisible
and dissipating. disagreeable. *transient . . .*
*less felt and sooner forgotten with them . . .*
*among the blacks is misery enough, god*
*knows, but no poetry.*[2]

did
you taste your sister's
lamentation on the wind,
streaming behind him like
wings? he flew away with her,
made you ride in his wake.
you held a razor to his neck
daily, scraping away protrusions.
did you think about it,
brother? did your mind wander,
traveling, thinking of Virginia and
the promised land of Dolly's
embrace, how she
proved him wrong daily?
did you ever see him leak red
from your errant twist of fingers,
did you know you came
well recommended? he went on trips
and couldn't find you. kept calling
you back to Monticello, he bet
you'd never run.

brother,
he was angry at the thought.
you, free, walking
brother, they said you *expressed great uneasiness*
*at having (ac)quitted* him *in the manner* you *did*
*and repeatedly declared*
*that* you *would never have left* him *to live*
*with any person but* your *wife.*[3]
*like you had a choice.*
*you were bearing a*
*curse, written in hot iron*
*and aimed at your neck,*
*a compliment, a new name,*
*Genteel.*

but you wriggled free
from his bitter
denigration onto decades
and your own land. died to
a gunshot ringing with bells,
the pastoral sprawl of
heaven opening up
with your last gasps,
an endless dawn.
he couldn't dream those last
twenty years. the
warm fingers of morning,
the rhythm of breath,
the lyric of your name,
life a poem
free of misery.

## NOTES

1. Thomas Jefferson, *Notes on the State of Virginia,* ed. Robert Forbes (New Haven, CT: Yale University Press, 2023), 264.

2. Jefferson, 264–267.

3. "Martha Jefferson Randolph to Thomas Jefferson, 15 January 1795," Founders Online, National Archives, https://founders.archives.gov/documents/Jefferson/01-28-02-0184. [Original source: John Catanzariti, ed., *The Papers of Thomas Jefferson,* vol. 28, 1 January 1794–29 February 1796 (Princeton, NJ: Princeton University Press, 2000), 246–247.]

# Founding and Finding Generational Archives

*A Conversation between Descendants of Monticello J. Calvin Jefferson Sr. and Jabari Jefferson with Auriana Woods*

*This conversation between grandfather and grandson—archivist J. Calvin Jefferson Sr. and artist Jabari Jefferson—participants in the* Declaration House *project, was recorded on March 11, 2025, on Zoom and moderated by Auriana Woods, director of the Getting Word African American History Department at Monticello.*

**Auriana Woods: Could you start by saying your name, your connection to Monticello, and telling us what your involvement was in the *Declaration House* project?**

**J. Calvin Jefferson Sr.:** My name is J. Calvin Jefferson Sr., and my connection with Monticello is through three families that were enslaved there.[1] Those families are the Evans family, from Jupiter, and his mother and father. And the Evanses started out at Shadwell with Peter Jefferson.[2] The second family is the Granger family, Ursula and George Granger. They were the first family that Thomas Jefferson and Martha Jefferson purchased when they got married. And the last family is the Hemings family. And the first Hemings that came to Monticello was my direct ancestor, Betty Brown Hemings. And she was the lady's maid for Martha Jefferson before she married Thomas Jefferson. And that's the connection that I have with Monticello and the Jefferson-Randolph family initially. There were people that were born at Monticello that are my ancestors.

I was introduced to Monument Lab and the *Declaration House* project by Gayle Jessup White. Initially, they thought that they could find descendants of Robert Hemmings, who was in Philadelphia at the time [of the signing of the Declaration of Independence], and we at Getting Word didn't have any [Robert] Hemmings descendants that we knew of. So, they broadened the search and decided to take photographs of the eyes of people who were descendants of the larger enslaved population at Monticello. I thought it was a worthy project because talking about Thomas Jefferson writing the Declaration of Independence, and how one of the people that was close to him during that period and that lived with him in Philadelphia happened to be an enslaved person who was related to his wife—that put a juxtaposition in talking about freedom. All men are created equal, yet one of the people that was serving you was an enslaved person.

**Jabari Jefferson:** Yeah, I could easily say ditto. My grandfather moved down there to Monticello, and me and my grandfather are very close. The Ford Foundation and the Thomas Jefferson Foundation [owner and operator of Monticello] commissioned me to do some work at Monticello in 2022. And so I have an original piece that was acquired by [Monticello] and housed in their permanent collection. It was unveiled to the public in a dual exhibition between me and the contemporary mixed-media artist Titus Kaphar. And then it just continued to build from there in different capacities. I was invited with my younger sibling and my grandfather to Philadelphia, initially not really understanding what the *Declaration House* project was about, but I learned that it was [led] by this artist, Sonya Clark, who was a fellow alumnus of [the School of the Art Institute of Chicago]. And then I was introduced to Monument Lab in Philadelphia—good people. That made me feel closer to the project, and a year later I was fortunate to be able to travel with my grandfather to go see it. I mean, of course the concept is wonderful, but what I was more inspired by was the artist Sonya Clark and how she's able to use her art practice to impact a city with the heritage of another place and merge history with contemporary art.

**AW: Jabari, in thinking about your artistic practice and your work, and then, Calvin, in thinking about your career as an archivist, from my point**

**of view, *Declaration House* brings your professions together. It uses archival photographs of your ancestors and folks that were enslaved in Monticello and their descendants. So, it has many elements of the archive but then, through Clark's artistic practice, it overlays your modern-day eyes over those archival eyes and uses that product to impact another city with the stories of Monticello. I would love to hear from both of you, from the point of view of your own distinct career paths. Calvin, could you talk a little bit about your work as an archivist and what that's looked like? And how do you think about *Declaration House* being in conversation with your career?**

**CJ:** Well, my career as an archivist is from the viewpoint of being an audiovisual archivist, meaning my specialty is film. I worked at the National Archives for about thirty-five years, but I was in the federal government for forty years. I started out as an archival technician in declassification, and then I became a technician in the motion-picture branch. Then, I became a union official before I became an archivist. I was also president of the American Federation of Government Employees Council 260. And when I became an archivist, I was still in the motion-picture branch. When the National Archives moved to College Park, I became the first supervisor of the research rooms at College Park. And from there, I ended up being in an office as a management analyst before I retired. So, I had a couple of positions in the National Archives, but to me, I have more stories and experiences in the motion-picture section because I met so many people that were actually making new movies. And some of them were nice, and some of them were crazy, but overall the experience was good.

What I see, the idea of art and history, they merge, because every time someone sees something historical, they imagine an image of that historical event. And the question is, how accurate is that image? What *Declaration House* has done is keep consistent with the accuracy of the images and telling the story. They're not manipulating the audience like some documentary filmmakers will do. They're giving you the information visually, and you must interpret it for yourself and see how it affects you. So, I think that they're doing a very good job of blending art with history. And I think over the years, since I've helped several filmmakers make new films, I know the process, and the process that I know is true to what's happening and telling the truth. And to me, with history, you have to be factual, and you don't deviate from the truth. The truth may hurt some people, but it's the truth, and that's what historical writing and imagery should be all about.

**AW: And what historical truth would you say that *Declaration House* was putting on display or trying to tell?**

**CJ:** What I took away from it is that they were showing images of people who were enslaved when the declaration was written. And by showing that, you can see expressions of their descendants today. That's kind of impactful, because some of the eyes are inquisitive eyes, some of them [a]re solemn. But to me, the project takes you back to that period of time—those emotions were probably some of the same things felt by the enslaved. The white colonists were talking about independence, talking about "all men are created equal," and then you had Robert Hemmings sitting there—he had to be scratching his head. If all men are created equal, then why was he enslaved? And believe me, they had a grapevine for talking to other enslaved people when they got back home. So, he was telling people what was going on in Philadelphia, too, I believe. I can't see enslaved people not talking about what was going on out there that was out of their control.

**AW: Jabari, could you talk a little bit about your work as an artist, your practice and how it came to be, and how you view your work in conversation with *Declaration House*?**

**JJ:** I'm a mixed-media artist based in Washington, D.C. I've been an artist since I was a child but have moved into a more formal painting practice that evolved into a mixed-media practice, which is just utilizing all aspects and objects within the work. As a mixed-media artist, it's about adding anything you want to your painting practice to give it more spirit. I'm classically trained from an academic point of view; I've attended the School of the Art Institute of Chicago as well as studied abroad in Italy. I've had residencies and different museum acquisitions. I've always been a full-time artist, which has allowed me to have a different relationship with my career. My work is Black figurative work that focuses on concepts of spirituality and history, but more so its relationship with the contemporary period and how these conversations are perceived through today's lens, whether they're forgotten about stories and you're reminding them of history or you're recontextualizing a narrative—a conversation that we're all familiar with. Which brings me to the installation that Monument Lab made in Philadelphia, which is pretty much the same concept. And that's what inspired me, the public nature of the piece. And when doing a public installation piece or something that is supposed to be reflective of a public, you have a lot of shareholders that you have to make happy, specifically if you're doing it and working with the city. So, the project seems to be taking a subject matter and just recontextualizing it. And it seemed like the strategy was to contextualize it with humanity rather than just have names in order to create some form of a tactic for the viewer to be able to translate that narrative into actual people. It uses the eye as a symbol, a symbol of the soul. And I think the coolest part of it is that it was juxtaposed within this somewhat stale area of history. Everything else historically in that period doesn't seem like it's been revised in the last fifty years of corrections and amendments and/or from a contemporary point of view. And that's why that piece stands out. It was just recontextualizing a stale narrative. I think the whole team—and specifically, I also just want to shine some light on Monument Lab and the overall responsibility it had as an entity with a narrative that was about re-creating monuments around the nation and finding funding for that to be able to give creators a platform to have a vision. And I know that they, as well as other people, were a big reason why this was able to occur, to bring in the artists to do something like that. And that's how I approached my work. That's how I approach the piece that Monticello commissioned, because from that standpoint, you have to engage regular Philadelphians that don't care or are just on their way to work. You have to make the people that you're representing in terms of the legacy and the families of the legacies happy. You've got to make sure the people that threw up the money are happy. You've got to make sure your own integrity as an artist and your practice is happy. So, you've got to wear a couple different hats and land in this place. And that's not always easy to do. And if you can do that and there's no complaints on it, everyone is just kind of smiling, then that's successful, especially because you've got to keep in mind that many people just don't care about art, don't care about you, don't care about history, and you still got to satisfy them as well. So, that's how I feel about it.

**AW: Calvin, could you tell the story of how you first came into a formal relationship with Monticello [and Getting Word]? What's the history of you connecting those dots and realizing that you're a descendant of this place?**

**CJ:** Well, I didn't connect the dots. The dots were connected by Lucia [Cinder] Stanton and Dianne Swann-Wright, and that's the way I met them.[3] It's interesting because my mother had a friend that she grew up with, and Cinder called my mother [in 1993], since my mother had the last name Jefferson, and said that people at Monticello were looking for descendants [of the enslaved community] and that we should call. Mother told me, and I called up Cinder and told her about the story of my great-grandfather, Robert Hughes, having a church down here [in Albemarle County] and being enslaved by Thomas Jefferson Randolph.[4] And at that time, Cinder said she didn't have any information on that. So, about two years later, I got a call from my cousin [confirming the story of my great-grandfather], and I said, "I knew it." So, I called [Cinder] then, and we talked about who Robert Hughes's mother was and who his grandmother was. And when she told me that his grandmother was Elizabeth Hemings, my mouth kind of dropped open because I didn't know I was related to Elizabeth Hemings at all. And then later on, Cinder told me she found out that Robert Hughes's wife, Sidney, was the granddaughter of Jupiter Evans. And she told me that Wormley Hughes's wife was Ursula [Granger], and she told me about the Granger family [of Monticello]. So, they gave me the information on who my ancestors were.

And from that point, I just read everything I could. And since then, I think Cinder and Dianne, they were trying very hard to stick with the facts of the people who were enslaved there. And they had some tussles with some people who wanted to kind of deviate from what the facts were. And then when Cinder retired, we had Niya [Bates], who did a very good job of keeping things up [as director of Getting Word]. But again, there are people that wanted to deviate from the facts. And she held the line on that by sticking with the facts. And the next person that in line [to be director] was Andrew [Davenport]. And here again, you're talking about a historian, and Andrew, he held the line on the facts also. But I look at my position [as an archival consultant] a little bit differently, since I'm older than everybody on staff. I consider myself in a position to teach as well as be a consultant because everybody's younger than I am, including the person that succeeded Andrew as director—she's younger, and I call her "Boss Lady" because she's the boss—

**AW: You're talking about me?**

**CJ:** Yes. And I want everybody to succeed because I know this is not going to be their last position in life. So, therefore, I try to give positive feedback on some of the things that they do so they can be successful. And if they're successful, that means the program is successful. And I think the program itself is doing a great job of telling people about the history not just of Monticello but the history of Virginia. And they're moving in the direction of that at the [Thomas Jefferson] Foundation each day, talking about Virginia. They're talking about the Native Americans that were in Albemarle County at the time. So, we're going beyond just the obvious at the foundation, and I'm very proud of that.

**AW: That's brilliant, Calvin. Thank you. You just brought so many things to mind, but I think I can say, well, I think most of the team—Jenna [Owens] and Ty'Leik [Chambers]—think of you as the grandfather of the project. I've told you many times before that you and my dad are the nearly same person and almost the same exact age, so I see you much more as a father figure. You are the elder of the project and someone that we listen to and joke on and joke with. And every once in a while, we might make fun of you a little bit. But I think you are one of the first people [at Monticello] that showed me that this work is family, and we might not all be directly connected to this place, but we are all connected to this story. I think seeing your truly familial relationship with Andrew [Davenport] and your relationship with the team showed me that the work [of Getting Word] can do more than just connect blood-related relatives. It can also form families from folks that all exist in the wake of slavery and are all connected to this story, and that doing this work is more than just work: It's doing work of and for our ancestors. And maybe they crossed paths, maybe they didn't, but they are all connected and related through these stories that we're telling and uncovering.**

**JJ:** I've been to Monticello a lot more than I ever would've thought. So, you can't go somewhere consistently without changing your relationship with it. I know when I first went there, I remember being very angry. It was actually infuriating; it was upsetting. And then that changed over time until a new perspective was formed. And then now, being on the board of certain things and just involved [with the foundation], I don't even think about those things anymore. I guess there's a sense of pride, and I think that came from my grandfather's relationship with the place and his enthusiasm, as well as how he's treated. And it is a real blessing. And yeah, I mean, I think I always count my blessings. I think I'm a very fortunate person in so many ways, particularly with the family that I've been bestowed, and I'm grateful to have my elders and to have a relationship with my grandparents and my great-grandparents on both sides of my father's line.

They all knew me, and even though they passed away when I was a kid, I was still old enough to know them and to have a conscious relationship with them and the things that they taught me. So sometimes, when you—and I call that "privilege"—so sometimes, when you are in a position of privilege, you consider it to be the norm. So, having a historian, multiple historians, in my family seemed normal. Having an elder that could trace generations back from my family was considered normal, or having a seriousness about history and being able to articulate it confidently was normal to me. It wouldn't be until I got older that it would be other people's reactions to me telling my family's history that allowed me to understand that it is actually *abnormal*. It's not the norm for people to be able to trace back their family and know how to do it using genealogy. It's not the norm to have accredited family members who've actually spent years on certain subject matters and can speak about it from an authoritative point of view. To be able to have your father be a public speaker and authoritative source on things, as well as your grandfather, and [Getting Word staff] at the same time is wonderful. We've normalized education in our family, not only what's taught in school but going above and beyond in your own personal time just because you can. And that all came from my grandfather's leadership, and I hope to continue that tradition.

**AW: I want to talk a little bit more about last names. Calvin, when Cinder first confirmed your connection to Monticello's enslaved community in 1995, was it surprising to you? Or did you already have a sense of it?**

**CJ:** It was a big shock. My mother didn't know anything. For me, when I got the information on who my family was, it's very interesting, especially the Hemings family. There's a lot written about them; in the letters that are in the archives of the foundation, people talk about the enslaved people. I found out more about my ancestors through [those letters] than from anything else.

And when I read how they describe some of the Hemings women, all I could think of was my mother. My mother had all these personality traits that Betty Brown had, and I was surprised at that. And today, thanks to scientific research, DNA, I've found other people I'm related to who I never thought I would be related to. And seeing how some of Elizabeth Hemings's descendants, what they've done in history, to me, it's kind of mind-boggling. And nobody has put that [all of that] together yet, on what her descendants actually did and what they took away from the people that enslaved them. Did any of their philosophies or ways [of thinking] filter down to them because of environment? So, that's kind of on my mind right now—I'm finding out through research that several of Elizabeth [Hemings]'s descendants were active in some type of civil rights movement before there was a civil rights movement and leadership positions, from pre-1860 to today. So, I've been very surprised at all that.

**AW: How would it have impacted you to know all of this as a kid, instead of finding out later in life?**

**CJ:** Well, I believe that genealogy is much more important to us than what we think. I think I would've had a different path in education if I had known [my ancestry earlier in life]. I really didn't care about education until I didn't want to get drafted. I think I would've looked at it totally differently and looked into more educational pursuits than I did. The thing that I know I did was introduce Jabari's father to people who were in the educational field to make sure he understood why education was important. And I think that really worked. In turn, he did the same thing with his kids. So, I think most families build on top of each generation, somehow. I think my mother's father's people kind of lost their way and didn't realize that they had something to build on until a family member in her generation did a very good job of building on the past. Some of the other family members didn't.

**AW: Calvin, could you give us a brief overview of the major families represented in Getting Word's work and how they're all connected and interrelated?**

**CJ:** Yeah, I can do that. There are six [core] families.[5] You have the Gillette family, which I'm also related to because the Gillette family married into the

Granger family. You have the Hubbard family, which I don't think I'm related to, but they're related to some of the Gillettes. You have the Evans family, which I'm related to, and they're also related to some of the Hubbards, and they're related to some of the Hemings[es]. That's three. Then, you have the Granger family—like I said, I'm related to the Granger family. I do know [that the Grangers are] related to some of the Gillettes, and they're related to the Hemings family and Hemings-Hughes family. Getting Word has looked at a couple of Evanses, but we [don't know yet] how [they descend from] Jupiter, but we believe that they are descendants of Jupiter, and that they ended up down in Alabama. The Evanses are also related to the Hemings-Hughes [family] through Sidney Evans, who is my great-great-grandmother. Of course, there's the Hemings family, who are also related to the Hern family, who are another big family from Monticello. Then, there's the Fossett family, who are also Hemingses.

So, that's that. And when you look at the individual families and the people that Getting Word has contacted and interviewed, they didn't fall through the cracks before or after 1860. So, if you want to learn more about the people who were enslaved and what happened to them, all you have to do is start studying the people who were at Monticello. I think [our work at Getting Word today] is doing a lot of that work—looking at what people did pre–Civil War and post–Civil War, and where they fell in society, in order to start looking at the truth of this country.

**AW: I want to talk a little bit more about y'all's family and the Jefferson last name. Could you tell a little bit of the origin story? Where does the Jefferson last name come from?**

**JJ:** Well, from what I know of, [that] was just fate. It was just fate. We have this lineage that's tied to these historical figures that happened to be named Jefferson, but [our last name] comes from other lines of our family [not descended from Monticello], such as everything that my grandfather mentioned in this introduction. And then those names were lost throughout time. And it just happened to be that my grandfather's father, my great-grandfather, came up under an adopted family whose name was Jefferson. And then that's how that name came back to be. And it just so happens that we have this legitimate connection to the [Jefferson] name on the other side of the family. Did I get that right, Granddad?

**CJ:** Oh, you got it right. And when I speak, the first thing I say is that my last name has nothing to do with my heritage at Monticello. And then growing up with the name Jefferson, to me it was a pain. It was a burden, but I accepted it.

**AW: In what ways was it a burden?**

**CJ:** Kids like to play around and tease a lot. So, having the name Jefferson, and they were trying to make something of it—growing up in D.C., you see the Jefferson Memorial and a lot of references to Thomas Jefferson. So, it was that kind of a burden. I didn't feel like being bothered with that. But today, as an adult, I play with it.

**JJ:** I like it.

**AW: What do you both like about it? What do you feel like it represents?**

**JJ:** I like that [in] my name, I got two *J*s in my name. I like that as an artist—it works really well for me. But no, I think it makes it easier to explain certain things. If our last name was Roberts or something, and I'm trying to explain [our connection to Monticello], then you can't hear it. But the symbolism of [the Jefferson name] makes it easier [to explain].

**AW: And I think that, Calvin, you do a very good job of letting people know that you are related to multiple families—not just the Hemingses but the Hughes[es] and the Grangers. You're always very inclusive, but you always say it how it is—it's never just one family.**

**CJ:** You got to keep it real.

**AW: How do you think about Thomas Jefferson himself? How do you think about Jefferson, the man, and what he represents in relation to your own lives and work with Getting Word?**

**CJ:** Well, to me, Jefferson is a whole lot more complicated than people want to admit. He's complicated on racial issues, he's complicated on political issues, and he's misquoted a lot. And in today's society, even in the beginning of the last Congress [in January 2025], the Speaker of the House [Mike Johnson] quoted a prayer that he said Jefferson used every day—that wasn't true. And the [Thomas Jefferson] Foundation had to let people know that it wasn't true. When you're talking about history, you have to look at all sides of Thomas Jefferson, and you have to give credit to what he did to form the building blocks of the country. Even going back to the Declaration of Independence, people do not talk about Jefferson criticizing slavery in a part that was left out of the declaration. So, he's a complicated person. But make no mistake—anytime you enslave other people, you're not a good guy. No matter how far you take it, you're just not a good guy. So, I look at him from that point of view, and I think people should look at him as a human being and not put him on a pedestal. And they should never say that he was a product of his time. I hate that statement too.

**JJ:** This is an artist that people are not super fond of, but I'm going to quote Kanye West. He said, "They rewrite history, I don't believe in yesterday," and that's how I look at all public figures or any narrative that's been presented to me. I happen to have been born in a time of clarity and transparency. And with every day that goes by, the dust continues to clear. And every time that happens, more and more of everything that you've been taught, you understand it's just strategic propaganda. And so that's how I feel about it.

**AW: What do you both feel about separating out Jefferson from Monticello? I think a lot of people might conflate the two: "The place is the man." When I think about the work [of Getting Word], Monticello is a place, and it is a representation of the over 610 people that lived and labored for it, at it, and all of their descendants. So, maybe a better question is: What does Monticello represent to you both personally, and also in your work and life? What do you see as its story and the power it might have?**

**CJ:** Well, for me, Monticello is Jefferson, and Jefferson is Monticello. And the reason I say that is because it's a reflection of the time period, and it is a reflection of a person who was more of an intellectual than a farmer, how he contributed to building a new country, and how he treated people that he enslaved. The treatment [of the people he enslaved] was uneven. I say the treatment was uneven [because] it's very clear that he favored [some people] because he emancipated them. And everyone that he emancipated was a descendant of Elizabeth Hemings. Same thing for those who were skilled laborers and got paid for some of [their work]. So, I think when you study Thomas Jefferson, you have to study the lives of the people he enslaved. That way, you get to understand the full person, and you put them into historical context. So, I don't think you can separate them. And I see the [Thomas Jefferson] foundation moving into a thought pattern of talking about the land, how the land was used, and how T. J. interacted with people. That's where I'm hoping that [the foundation] keeps on going with the narrative of Monticello. And I'm hoping that the descendants become a little bit more active and a little bit more constructive with their conversation and criticism about how things are reflected to the general public.

**JJ:** The one thing I think is very interesting about Monticello is it sits on a lot of power, a lot of unacknowledged power, because it's the literal [birthplace] of an ideology. [The foundation] is a whole institution that focuses on a subject matter that [is] at the bedrock of this country. So, everything that moves forward from there, whether you look at today's politics, it all sits on this narrative and the institution happens to be the primary source of this narrative. But what's special is how Monticello is taking an unprecedented initiative to [tell that narrative in full], and it is a bit of an anomaly in that way. It intends to produce a narrative [that is more nuanced] than the traditional story, and it then attracts minds that are aligned with that intention.

But you can do positive things and then receive backlash from other people that's like, what are they doing up there? They're shifting this narrative. They're focusing on something different. Little do they know, they're interrupting a foundational story to allow other stories to be told, to tell a fuller story. And if they continue to do what they're doing and are successful in that, you're [widening] the fabric of this nation. I think that's the importance that all of these characters are playing in this time period at this location.

**AW: I couldn't agree more. I often talk about Monticello as a metaphor in the sense that it represents all of the institutions, the people, and the forces that shaped this country. And if you take a good, hard look at it, you see that it is a history and a place that is just as Black as it is red, white, and blue. And that this site of American history is a site of African American history—that the two are inextricable.**

**In thinking about Monticello as a monument, and also Declaration House as a monument, could you define what a monument is to you? It might be more than a building, it might not be a building at all, it might be a person, but could you talk about your definition of the word?**

**CJ:** I never thought about it as something different than an object. The conception of a monument to me is, I guess it's really having a hero. A lot of heroes don't have monuments, you have thoughts about them, and it's a mental picture of someone or something or some activity to be a monument. If you do have a monument that's a building, it has to have significance to me. And you shouldn't have to think about what the significance is. It should be an "in-your-face" type thing. And what they did at Monument Lab, they re-created the building where the Declaration of Independence was written, and then they put the eyes up there, and that tells you a story that is an untold story. But as a monument itself, it's a little bit different because, keep in mind, some monuments are not monuments. They may be monuments to one segment of the population. It kills me when they talk about the statues of the Confederate generals, how when they came down that people were taking down monuments of their history. Well, hell, every time I went and saw those things, it was negative to me.

**AW: So how do you view "The Descendants of Monticello"? Was that a monument to you?**

**CJ:** That is a monument to me because they included the descendants—or the eyes of the descendants—of people who were not treated equal when the declaration was written. And to me, that's the story. All men are created equal, and ever since 1865, that's where the country has tried to go. But every time it takes one step forward, it takes three steps back. That's why you have all this stuff going on today—you have people trying to take away birthright citizenship, which was meant to promote equality. It's just crazy.

**AW: Jabari, as an artist and also as a descendant—what is a monument to you?**

**JJ:** Well, one thing I love about art is that it deals with symbolism. The reason pictures and 2D objects are actually more powerful than sound and a lot of other [mediums] is because you're dealing with symbolism. And symbolism is one of the most profound things in an individual's consciousness. This is what you remember, even when you don't remember. So, you're dealing with the subconscious, and through the subconscious, you can implement things without the conscious mind being aware of it. You can think things and remember things that come to you, and you don't even really understand why. And so you have these ideas, these expressions, and without it being encased in something, it's just spirit. So, it's the spirit in the room, the spirit of the times, and it's not until that spirit is encased in something that it is real. And a monument is that spirit encased in something. So, now it actually exists. It's this tangible thing that is functional—it's doing something. In today's Western culture, we look at monuments and art and things as this decorative thing. But traditionally and from an Indigenous standpoint, these things and encasements that were made were all meant to be functional. The aesthetic of it was like secondary, tertiary, but it was meant to be performative. It was meant to actually do something. This is why we made it. And that's what the idea of a monument is: It is to do something. And it's not about good or bad or, in my opinion, right side of history, wrong side of history. It's just more willpower. I believe in this. I had the will to execute it, and there it is. And most times, that monument outlives the people that initially made it. And so it's always in the reaction of whoever is living at the times and what they decide to do with it. Do they decide to continue this narrative? Do they decide to promote it? Do they decide to celebrate it, or have times changed? Laws change, rulers change, mindsets change, and now, we want to part ways from it or recontextualize it, which is what they did in Philadelphia [with *Declaration House*].

**AW: I want to end by talking a little bit about *Declaration House* as a project. And I know we've touched on it a little bit, but I was here when y'all were getting your pictures taken and the recording of your eyes. But I would love to hear a little bit about the experience that y'all had, seeing it in person.**

**CJ:** Well, when I saw it the first time, I was overwhelmed, and I couldn't recognize anybody's eyes. But I just thought it was, it was overwhelming, and the eyes changed in the windows, and I watched the audience look at it. And I talked to a couple of people both times [I saw the exhibit], and I went up there when they first opened up, and I went up when Jabari and I talked to people in the audience, too, and they seemed to be overwhelmed by the project also. And one of my good buddies came down the first time to see it, and he and his wife—they're both archivists—they liked it too. They thought it was overwhelming. And his wife is from Philly, so it kind of had a different meaning to her because she grew up in Philly. So, I just thought it was beautiful. I thought it was something that was very, very appropriate for the time. And it would be great if they kept it up until next year, July 4.

**JJ:** I just enjoy the execution of it all. I think it allowed me to have more empathy for and just to better understand the audience, when a creator is trying to explain something, but [the audience] can't truly see it. They can hear you, but they can't envision it, and no one can really envision it other than the visionary. And so it felt good to be on the other side of that. We took the pictures. Cool. And then you see it and it's like, oh man, *this* is what you was talking about. Oh, *this* is the vision you had. And I think what was more memorable for me was just seeing other people's interactions with it—not just people who were aware of the historical aspect [of the project] but just regular Philadelphia citizens at a bus stop in front of a Dunkin' Donuts, probably getting on the bus, coming home from work or something, and they're just watching it and trying to figure out what's going on, and there's this new thing that's on their traditional work route that maybe creates a moment of getting out of the mundane of what they're used to seeing. You interrupted their normal tradition with something cool. And being able to see that on the people's faces was memorable.

**AW: What was it like for you two, as grandson and grandfather, to be involved in this project together? Do you feel like it impacted your relationship at all?**

**CJ:** It just reinforced our relationship. And keep in mind, there was another grandchild too. Jade was with us, and I think as [Jade and Jabari] grew up, they got immersed with their family history. When I say "their family history," not just from my side but from their dad's mother's side and from their other parent's side too. So, they had an introduction to what it means to know who you are. So for me, it just added to the relationship I had with both my grandkids.

**JJ:** And for me, just another day in the life of my grandfather.

**AW: Y'all got [printed] portraits of yourselves from Monument Lab? Can you talk a little bit about them? What do you think about them, and what did they symbolize for you?**

**CJ:** I thought they were great. I just have to find a place on my wall for them. I was sitting down, Jabari's on one side, Jade's on the other side. It is a nice portrait, and each one of us got one.

**JJ:** Yeah, I think I like my grandfather's the most. He has a lot of good characteristics in his face. I feel like you recognize him in his eyes and his smile, and that kind of stuff is more important to me.

**AW: Yeah, he's quite the picture taker, your granddad, he takes a good picture.**

**JJ:** Very photogenic.

**AW: Well, thank you both. Is there anything else that you want to touch on or say about *Declaration House*?**

**CJ:** No, I'm good.

**JJ:** Yeah, I think this was incredibly thorough. I don't think there was really any stone left unturned.

**AW: Oh, trust me, there's always stones left unturned with Mr. Jefferson, but I think we got most of it. We got at the root of it.**

## NOTES

1. The families J. Calvin Jefferson Sr. refers to are the Evans family, through Jupiter (1743–1800); the Grangers, through George and Ursula's second son, Bagwell (1768–1827+); and the Hugheses, through Elizabeth Hemings's daughter Betty Brown and her second son, Wormley Hughes (1781–1827+). Bagwell's daughter Ursula married Wormley, and their son Robert Hughes married Sidney Evans, Jupiter's granddaughter. Robert Hughes and Sidney Evans are J. Calvin Jefferson Sr.'s maternal great-great-grandparents.

2. Situated on the northern bank of the Rivanna River, Peter Jefferson acquired Shadwell in the late 1730s. The plantation was inherited by his son Thomas Jefferson, who in turn deeded it to his grandson Thomas Jefferson Randolph in 1813. In the late 1820s, following the death of Jefferson, Randolph purchased many members of the Granger and Hughes families, and they would eventually come to live on an adjoining property called Edgehill, also owned by Randolph. Both properties are located at the junction of Routes 250 and 22 in Keswick, Virginia.

3. The Getting Word African American History Department at Monticello was founded in 1993 by Senior Historian Emeritus Lucia [Cinder] Stanton and former director of African American Special Programs at Monticello Dianne Swann-Wright.

4. In November 1867, Thomas Jefferson Randolph deeded one acre "at the intersection of the Turnpike Gap Road [Louisa Road/Rt. 22], and the Richmond Road [Rt. 250] . . . for the purpose of building a church and School House for the said Union Branch Baptist Congregation." The deed lists the deacons of what would later be known as Union Run Baptist Church; among those named were George Hughes and Lewis Hern. George's brother Robert Hughes would be one of the churches' founding ministers. Prior to the Civil War, an earlier church had been established at Shadwell in a slave cabin located in the hills above the plantation ("Robert Hughes," Getting Word African American History Department Archive, Levy-Era Families series, Box 14, Folder 149 [Charlottesville, VA: Thomas Jefferson Foundation]).

5. Presently, the six families from the enslaved Monticello and Poplar Forest communities that form the core of Monticello's public interpretation of slavery are Evans, Gillette, Granger, Hemings/Hemmings, Hern/Hearnes, and Hubbard.

# Blinking Black Urbanism

## *Placesteading in the Fictions of Philadelphia's Seventh Street and Declaration House*

Matthew J. M. Kenyatta

### I. Black Urbanism as Placesteading in the Margins

When I was age eight, the Underground Railroad made its first stop in my imagination, mapped in the pages of a secondhand Harriet Tubman biography. My grandmother—a cotton-picking working-class daughter of Arkansas who'd migrated to California—rescued it from a garage sale. Even with gum stuck to its pages, I read it cover to cover. I learned how the abolitionist conductor and military strategist became the fledgling nation's ultimate wayfinder: bravely charting an Afrofuturist landscape by traveling distances as formidably as John Muir, but with the spirit of Moses. Knowing this history makes it even more curious why African Americans are often omitted from affirming narratives about place in the United States.

I have spent much of my career navigating such cultural sites as Declaration House—places where Black presence is footnoted and decentered as their norm. In the summer of 2024, as a Diversity, Equity, and Inclusion Fellow through Dumbarton Oaks and Harvard University, I toured another such site: the University of Virginia (UVA), designed by Thomas Jefferson. Yet again, I found myself moving through a place that demands all forms of attention and resources to be summoned for its worship. Even our dismay and disgust become sustenance for its politely persistent narcissism.

The long, sweaty tour was led by a professor at UVA's architecture school, who was deeply invested in offering an anti-colonial reenactment of enslavement, encyclopedically narrating its horrors in a way that was rehearsed, neat, and predictable. These publicly photographed performances of reckoning often obscure more than they reveal. By dutifully reciting canonical texts and failing to critically fabulate about their gaps, these tours can render whoever was silenced—e.g., the Hemings family of Monticello—as ghosts in the master narrative of Jefferson.

While I did not have many positive experiences in that laborious visit to UVA's Academical Village, one moment sticks with me: As we stood in the back of the Colonnade Club dormitories near the headmasters' original homes—spaces deliberately interwoven into the central campus—the guide pointed out the gardens built with low walls, just high enough to hide the enslaved labor happening behind them. The serpentine curvature patterns and wild, seemingly organic landscaping choices softened the severity of captivity, making enslavement easy to look past.

I asked the guide: What would that have felt like for the enslaved laborers moving through these hidden spaces? Was there any sense of dreaming, of an alternative sacred geography? Did these backlots—these cloaked spaces of labor—ever function as an undercommons? Undercommons, as Fred Moten once meant it, are hidden spaces to operate plans for securing sovereign places in the world, places of "means without ends, of love among things," places of "conservation . . . rest . . . gathering, cooking, drinking, and smoking," as fugitivity against governed labor; places for "the ongoing amplification of the bottom"; places for "the ceaseless experiment with the futural presence of the forms of life that make such activities possible": essentially, places for abolition and reconstruction. I wasn't interested in rehashing suffering for suffering's sake; I wanted to challenge the guilt and vanity of rehearsing brokenness as an endpoint, to make space for learning how "the multitude is already productive for itself," how an undercommons "uses every quiet moment, every sundown, every moment of militant preservation [of integrity], to plan together, to launch, to compose (in) its surreal time."[1] Compunction is an aperture that cannot witness the ancestral genius behind resilience.

I was reminded of this tension in 2019 when I was invited to a live taping of Oprah's premiere of Ta-Nehisi Coates's debut novel, *The Water Dancer*, in Washington, D.C., at the Carnegie Library—an Apple-owned site itself wrapped in twenty-first-century contradictions of preservation and commerce. With the book, each attendee was given free tickets to Monticello—the very plantation that inspired the novel's speculative landscape of memory, resistance, and enslavement. The pandemic intervened so I never used my tickets. Even if it hadn't, I doubt that I would have gone voluntarily.

Not because I am fragile but because I am fed up.

I tire of living in a place that centers white colonialists with a steep price tag: our collective footnoting of Black interiority and dignified spatial imaginarie. What if that very hierarchy is isolating Declaration House from broader stewardship possibilities? What if the local disengagement around Declaration House prior to this artistic intervention stems from that same disinterest—the utter lack of curiosity about the wider populations who made this democracy possible? What if a beautiful array—the entire rainbow of distinctive truths—awaits the bold world beyond this same fortressed dynamic that has long rendered Black placemaking invisible, Black permanence untenable, and Black belonging provisional?

Thankfully, I bear witness to underground truths surfacing in public. As an art commissioner, I celebrated my thirty-fourth birthday by approving the City of Philadelphia's first commissioned monument of a specific Black woman: this "woman called Moses." Tubman's coming sculpture joins that of abolitionist Octavius Catto (2017) in the long-overdue exodus from a monumental landscape that has marginalized Black Philadelphians. Yet like Moses, these traditional monuments can only lead us so far, pointing toward but not entering a promised land of cultural recognition. Philly has wandered for decades between stale narratives of placekeeping and gentrified spectacles of placemaking.

Enter Sonya Clark. With her installation of a video-based piece with a divergent story—one about Black history not merely coexisting with but fundamentally shaping American history—Clark's "The Descendants of Monticello" becomes our Joshua, boldly tilling new territory through what I call "placesteading." *Placesteading* is the act of producing culture and sustaining neighborhood economies without equitable support from propertied institutions. It is a mode of Black urbanism that exists in the shadows of spatial abandonment, resisting erasure while lacking official recognition or structural protection. Placesteading is not just survival—it is a strategic form of counter-valuation, insisting that presence and cultural production hold value beyond what is acknowledged by formal markets or urban planning frameworks. Much like the street economies of Black urban districts whose placemakers sustain vitality without formal ownership, this installation engages in placesteading—momentarily reorienting the power dynamics of a space that otherwise resists Black presence.

## II. Blinking, Biking, Walking: Personal Encounters with Declaration House's Descendants

Being a bicyclist, my relationship to Philadelphia's streetscape is intimate. I think in landmarks and ease of movement when defining what an "attraction" is. Because I exist in an intersectional prismatic body—Black, queer, male, formally educated—I also think about what evokes a sense of unbothered belongingness. What might allow for an aliveness just as I am?

As a Los Angeles scholar adopted by Philadelphia, I carry a perspective shaped by Black spatial imaginaries across different cities. Black urbanism isn't just about spaces being historically Black but about the lived strategies—policies, preservation, placemaking practices—of making them *feel* Black in the present. On September 27, 2024, months after the "The Descendants of Monticello" public art installation debuted, I decided to return to an intersection I'd paid little attention to during my seven years in this city: Seventh and East Market Streets.

I've visited Declaration House on three occasions during this installation. Once was in July at its opening celebration—an approachable yet spectacular gathering of Philadelphia's artistic and civic leaders, with jazz singers, monument swag, vox populi–filmed interviews, speeches, and tours. But this essay is not about that day. In fact, that day serves as a contrast to elucidate what could be versus what was.

One could be forgiven for feeling as though walking down this street is like entering a hush harbor—frozen in time, silenced, forgotten. I am sitting with the experience of a Dunkin' Donuts shop, with its pumpkin-colored cracked Liberty Bell logo, carrying more of the everyday attention economy than the historic site itself. Prior to Clark's intervention with Monument Lab at the blessing of the Thomas Jefferson Foundation and the National Park Service, being in this context was to know that Dunkin' Donuts draws more active attention than this foundational site of American democracy. While waiting to join a tour, I bought a meal for an unhoused person who had offered to hold the door—a small interaction that speaks volumes about the current socioeconomic landscape of this historically significant space.

In my walking adventures around Declaration House, I scanned for additional signs pointing toward this supposedly auspicious landmark. Instead, I found bus-stop kiosks highlighting the importance of Eighth and Market, with a historical photo of the Lit Brothers department store boasting "On This Day in 1898." Below the before-and-after pictures, several "events" blend Black excellence with commercial successes: Paul Robeson's birthday is listed alongside Hattie McDaniel's Oscar win, the introduction of Pepsi-Cola, and the death of Underground Railroad leader Robert Purvis.

Like Purvis's complex mixed-race lineage and his notable refusal to "pass" as white, this American history resists simple narratives of progress. It reveals blinking patterns: moments of luminous advancements and midnight retreats, moments of breakthroughs and backlashes, moments of cresting surges and ebbing undertows. On this same block, the Lit Brothers building (celebrated on these signs, yet closed in 1977 due to financial hardships) now hosts an anti-immigrant, anti-democracy campaign that projects messages onto the ruins of several cultural institutions under its forensic, blinding light. Yet we blink.

## III. Reading between the Dotted Lines of Erasure and Presence on Seventh and Market

How might one come to know the Declaration House as a pedestrian or a visitor when it reads "permanently closed" on a map? Or when its name is also scratched off the vinyl of a blade sign on the corner? If you happen to resist its digital and physical denouement, the bus stop's broadside poster and Declaration House building still greet you—but you cannot enter its doors. The generous newspaper-bound exhibition map provided at Monument Lab's summer block party and throughout the exhibition reveals seventeen surrounding landmarks between Franklin Square and Washington Square, each telling its own story of Black urban experience.

"[Placemaking] is the continual renewal of desacralized Black Space into newly sacralized Black Space to love and attention and community."[2] Theaster Gates's definition resonates deeply here, where the geography tells a story of equidistant possibilities. Declaration House straddles multiple place brands: Chinatown and Franklin Square to the north, Washington Square to the south, City Hall to the west, Old City and Society Hill to the southeast. In reading a map from north to south, you begin on Race Street, then Arch (which feels like *architecture*), and then you land on Market. This map communicates subliminally that race prefigures and builds an arch to a unique kind of market. The site stands between a federal detention center to the north and the original home of the African American Museum in Philadelphia to the south—a physical manifestation of our ongoing struggle between carcerality and freedom.

As I blink at the geographic patterns and fitful fractals of competing information around me, I wonder about intersections, vertices, and the grids of a neighborhood—the Philadelphia-born matrix of power and contradictory yet coexisting truths yearning to claim it as their destination. Are such places the permacultural grounds we still need to till to wrestle over democracy? The summer Trump advertisements blaring from the Lit Brothers rooftop across the street above the Declaration House seemed to think so. Below this cornice, the blade signs in deep blue and cherry red point to every destination besides Declaration House: Jewelers' Row, Independence Hall, Old City, shops, and more. Across the street, a teal and purple blade sign erected by Walk!Philadelphia points pedestrians in multiple directions for various attractions: Fashion District, Chinatown, African American Museum, Washington Square West, Free Library's Independence Branch, Chestnut/Walnut shopping.

The information architecture on these kiosks and environmental graphics tells an aspirational story of Philadelphia's commercial and civic past. But the omissions are just as loud as the inclusions. Much like the exclusion of Black urban neighborhoods from official narratives in tourism and destination marketing, Black presence here is mapped only in oblique references—never central, only as passing mentions designed to fade.

## IV. Democracy's Marginalia: The Right to Belong amid Competing Mythologies

At its core, this essay is about the right to belong—within historical narratives and in everyday spatial realities that last. To walk this block is to experience a tension between the fantasy of America's founding and the realities of its exclusions. Placesteading is an act of defying propertied exclusion—of stewarding space within that tension. If democracy is still being written, then Black urbanism is its marginalia, its countertext, its unblinking gaze.

By bridging digital and material realms as Sonya Clark has, we can ensure that Black presence in such places as Market Street is neither frozen in the past nor erased in the present. This physical, digital, and phygital preservation extends Black urbanists' tradition of reinterpreting history on our own terms. Just as digital world-building enables new cultural visibility, such installations as Clark's "blinking eyes" bring digital consciousness into historical erasure—asserting Black visibility in a city that continuously renders it ghostly.

At Seventh and Market, despite competing blade signs and scratched-off identities, Clark's installation created an equilibrium—where the descendants' blinking eyes reminded us of who else was present in the founding; who, too, shaped this democracy; and who also deserves more than the marginal notes history has assigned them. Yet standing here, one witnesses a contemporary palimpsest where a Dunkin' Donuts, a federal detention center, and the Declaration House somehow coexist as a living metaphor for democracy's unfinished work. A new declaration will not be written with quill and parchment, but perhaps it will be seen with the unblinking eyes of those who have witnessed America's promises and seek to reconcile its contradictions right on their block.

## NOTES

1. Stefano Harney and Fred Moten, *The Undercommons: Fugitive Planning and Black Study* (Brooklyn: Minor Compositions, 2013), 75, 77, 81, 82.

2. Theaster Gates, "Sacralized Space: Theaster Gates on the Practice of Placemaking," interview by Nu Goteh and Alice Grandoit-Šutka, *Deem*, no. 4 (Winter 2022/23): 16, https://deemjournal.com/sacralized-space-theaster-gates-on-the-practice-of-placemaking.

# Afterword

# "We Bind Ourselves Firmly by the Present"

## *Robert Hemmings's Progeny and Progress*

Salamishah Tillet

On August 28, 1812, Robert Hemmings, the first son of Virginia slaveholder John Wayles, Thomas Jefferson's father-in-law, and the enslaved woman Elizabeth Hemings, made sure to write himself and his progeny into history.

For many white Americans in Richmond, the document of a marriage bond was familiar enough. This one, costing $150 and made to cement the union between Hemmings's eldest daughter, Elizabeth, and her future husband, William Scott, was far rarer.[1] For Hemmings, who was born into slavery in 1762, and was, at age eleven, inherited by Jefferson when Jefferson's father-in-law, Wayles, died in 1773, the marriage license symbolized his radical shift in social standing.

His signature not only enshrined his position as a free Black man in Virginia but also ensured the passing down of that legal status (one shared by his wife, Dolly) to their daughter, her children, and several generations into the future, making it more than fitting for the artist Sonya Clark to name her monumental remembering of Hemmings's legacy of living in and working as Jefferson's teenage valet in Philadelphia in 1775 and again in 1776 "The Descendants of Monticello."[2]

Located at a bustling corner in Old City in the summer of 2024, "The Descendants of Monticello" was housed at the historic site Independence National

Historical Park's Declaration House, the home where Jefferson stayed while writing the Declaration of Independence. More specifically, Clark's artwork was a series of video screens in the building's windows that projected the eyes of Hemmings's progeny alongside those of other descendants of the more than four hundred people enslaved at Monticello.

"Robert Hemmings's descendants will have his eyes in there somewhere," Clark said, in an interview with the *Guardian*. "In the same way that you might have your great-uncle's or great-grandmother's eyes or hands or nose, the genetic stuff of him would be in his descendants."[3]

Unlike Jefferson's more than half a dozen life portraits, there are none of Hemmings. The earliest mentions of Hemmings's existence are found only in Jefferson's plantation ledger and personal letters. Later records include a deed of manumission in 1794, property fines, Richmond's poll taxes for his livery and hauling business, and, of course, the marriage bond.

While it is unsurprising that so little information about or by Hemmings exists in the public record, this lack is telling. The dearth of documents about formerly enslaved African Americans, including even those who were more coveted by Jefferson, such as the Hemings family, is a stark reminder of how many stories have been excised out of American history, and of how, ultimately, and unfairly so, it has been left up to the family members to keep their memory alive across generations, as well as artists, such as Clark, to fill in these historical gaps with creativity and complexity.

Now, with this edited collection titled *Declaration House*, we have another opportunity to pay homage to Hemmings. In these pages, scholars, poets, cultural leaders, and curators have come together to meditate on the meaning of Hemmings, as a child born into perpetual servitude; as a twelve-year-old handpicked by Jefferson to replace his thirty-one-year-old valet, Jupiter Evans; and as a self-made man who, through ingenuity, hard work, and foresight, years later secured his freedom and that of his wife.

Much like the spirit of Clark's "The Descendants of Monticello," this book bears witness to Hemmings's service to a young nation on the brink of democracy, even as at the same time, the country remained, as his bondage to Jefferson attests, deeply steeped in slavery.

These contributions also underscore the unique conditions under which Jefferson wrote the Declaration of Independence and finally give the public a chance to grieve the fourteen-year-old Hemmings, who was taken away from his family and all that was familiar in Virginia to attend to Jefferson's daily whims in Philadelphia.

This testament strives to match the scale of sacrifice. Monument Lab knew as much when its team commissioned Clark for this project, and Clark knew as much when she adorned the entire building in one of the most-visited neighborhoods in Center City with pairs of eyes that blinked, mesmerized, and engaged those walking by. Even more luminescent at night, Declaration House filled the street, beckoning those who stumbled upon it—or, like me, deliberately made a nocturnal pilgrimage to the site—to come closer. The intimacy enabled us to see ourselves and our histories reflected through the eyes of these descendants.

The young Robert Hemmings knew nothing of this legacy when he accompanied Jefferson to Philadelphia. But that did not mean he did not understand the meaning of freedom, a pursuit he dedicated his life to and, ultimately, through persuasion and proximity to Jefferson, achieved.

Perhaps more than anything, this book, like Clark's "The Descendants of Monticello," upon which it is based, stands next to his signature as a sprawling statement. Likely written with his nondominant hand (he lost the other after a shooting accident years earlier), his name appears substantive and definitive, further valorizing his literacy.[4] But by adding an extra *m* to his surname and that of his daughter Elizabeth, Hemmings differentiated himself from Jefferson—or, at least, the version that Jefferson had controlled until that point in print and thus, for so long, in American history.

A certain line jumps out to me every time I read the marriage bond: "We bind our heirs, executors, and administrators, jointly and severally, to the present." Sealed with paternal signatures, the certificate was an oath, for sure, but I also understand it as a promise for progress—one that Hemmings gave to his progeny, that Clark captured in the present, and that we, with our diverse perspectives about the past, continue to pledge here today.

## NOTES

1. In 2023, historians from Monticello's Getting Word African American History Department rediscovered Hemmings's signature, a revelation that they said confirmed "the literacy and the agency of the man that Thomas Jefferson enslaved as his valet." See Thomas Jefferson's Monticello, "Robert Hemmings's Signature," August 30, 2024, https://www.monticello.org/exhibits-events/livestreams-videos-and-podcasts/robert-hemmings-ichepod/.

2. David Smith, "Public Artwork Reframes US History of Enslavement through Jefferson's Valet," *Guardian*, June 27, 2024, https://www.theguardian.com/artanddesign/article/2024/jun/27/descendants-of-monticello-slavery-sonya-clark-philadelphia.

3. Smith.

4. Andrew M. Davenport, "Robert Hemmings's Declaration of Independance," in *Declaration House*, ed. Anna Arabindan-Kesson, Paul M. Farber, and Yolanda Wisher (Philadelphia: Temple University Press, 2026), 6.

# Acknowledgments

We offer profound gratitude to all the contributors to the *Declaration House* book and exhibition project.

**CREDITS**

**Lead Artist:** Sonya Clark

**Curatorial and Editorial Team:** Anna Arabindan-Kesson, Paul M. Farber, and Yolanda Wisher

**Exhibition and Book Project Managers:** Kerry Bickford, Amelia Carter, and Elliot Waters-Fleming

**Lead Partners:** Independence National Historical Park, Thomas Jefferson Foundation's Monticello and its Getting Word African American History Department

**Programmatic Partners:** African American Museum in Philadelphia, Fletcher Street Urban Riding Club, Free Library of Philadelphia, Harriet's Bookshop, Independence Historical Trust, Independence Visitor Center, Lenapehoking Reestablishment Project, Mural Arts Philadelphia, PhillyCAM, Wawa Welcome America, and WHYY

**Creative Residents:** Jeannine A. Cook and Ty "Dancing Wolf" Ellis

**Research Advisor:** Sue Mobley

**Documentation:** MING Media, Daniel Jackson, AJ Mitchell, Evan Morsell, and Steve Weinik

**Design:** Connie Harvey and Blair Richardson (MiniSuper Studio) and William Roy Hodgson

**Monument Lab Team:** Kareal Amenumey, Maya Björnson, Caro Campos, Justin Geller, Kristen Giannantonio, Jonai Gibson-Selix, Florie Hutchinson, Mecca Jones, Jennifer McTague, Naima Murphy Salcido, Allison Nkwocha, Aubree Penney, Stephani Pescitelli, Julie Rhoad, Bella Rodriguez, Dina Paola Rodriguez, Nico Rodriguez, Cleary Rubinos, Kate Sullivan, Yannick Trapman-O'Brien, and Steve Weinik

**Interns:** Steve Baron, Hannah Fisher Gray, and Danielle Degon Rhodes.

**Monument Lab Board of Directors:** Lola Bakare (Secretary), Chris Bavitz, Ellery Roberts Biddle (Co-Chair), Amari Johnson (Vice Chair), Rinku Modi, Monica O. Montgomery, Stephan Nicoleau (Treasurer), Michelle Angela Ortiz (Co-Chair), Samala, Kirk Savage, Tiffany Tavarez (Board Emerita), and Max Walden

**Special Thanks:** Laurie Allen, Niya Bates, Ty'Leik Chambers, Chisom Chieke, Andrew M. Davenport, Michael DelBene, Suzanne Holt, Daniel Jackson, Aaron Javsicas and the Temple University Press team, J. Calvin Jefferson Sr., Jane Kamensky, Jon Kaufman, Jenna Owens, El Sawyer, Superintendent Steven Sims and the staff of Independence National Historical Park, Gayle Jessup White, Nicole Allen White, Gabriel Wiener, Amber Wiley, Auriana Woods, and the many more people who made this project possible.

**Major support** for *Declaration House* has been provided by the Pew Center for Arts & Heritage, with additional support from VIA Art Fund and the National Endowment for the Arts. Lead project partners include Independence National Historical Park and the Thomas Jefferson Foundation's Monticello and its Getting Word African American History Department. Additional in-kind support has been provided by Wawa Welcome America, A2aMEDIA, and Clear Channel Outdoor.

# Image Credits

**Page a:** Detail from photo by Blair Richardson / MiniSuper Studio and Connie Harvey.
**Page 40:** Image courtesy of Gayle Jessup White.
**Page 41:** Image courtesy of Sonya Clark.
**Page 45:** *Top*: Image courtesy of Robert M. Skaler Postcard Collection/Athenaeum of Philadelphia. *Bottom*: Image courtesy of the Library of Congress.
**Page 46:** Image courtesy of the Thomas Jefferson Papers at the Library of Congress.
**Page 47:** Image courtesy of The New York Public Library.
**Page 48:** Image courtesy of the Library of Virginia.
**Page 49:** *Top*: Photo by Anthony Bernato, courtesy of Temple Digital Collections. *Bottom*: Photo by Daniel Jackson/Monument Lab.
**Pages 50–55:** Photos by Ashley J. Mitchell/Monument Lab.
**Page 56:** Photo by Ashley J. Mitchell/Monument Lab and Evan Morsell/MING Media.
**Page 57:** Production by Evan Morsell, Jon Kaufman, Chisom Chieke, El Sawyer, Sherly Rosario. Post-production by Alex Nguyen, Gabriel Wiener, Chisom Chieke.
**Pages 58–60:** Photos by Steve Weinik/Monument Lab.
**Page 61:** Photo by Daniel Jackson/Monument Lab.
**Pages 62–65:** Photos by Steve Weinik/Monument Lab.
**Page 66:** Image courtesy of Monument Lab.
**Page 67:** Photo by Terrell Halsey.
**Page 71:** Still courtesy of the Thomas Jefferson Foundation.

# Editors and Contributors

## EDITORS

Professor **Anna Arabindan-Kesson** works as a writer, curator, and associate professor of Black diasporic art at Princeton University. Before she began her Ph.D., she worked as a registered nurse in Australia; Aotearoa, New Zealand; and the U.K. Her prize-winning monograph *Black Bodies, White Gold: Art, Cotton, and Commerce in the Atlantic World* was published in 2021 with Duke University Press. She is an elected member of the American Antiquarian Society and a member of the Society of Fellows of the American Academy in Rome, and she directs Art Hx, a platform for exploring the convergences of art and medicine.

As the director and a cofounder of Monument Lab, **Paul M. Farber** is among the nation's thought leaders on monuments, memory, and public space. Farber is the author and a coeditor of several publications, including *A Wall of Our Own: An American History of the Berlin Wall* (2020), *Monument Lab: Creative Speculations for Philadelphia* (2020), and *National Monument Audit* (2021). His forthcoming book, *After Permanence: The Future of Monuments,* will be published with the University of North Carolina Press. Farber's curatorial and collaborative work includes *Beyond Granite: Pulling Together* with Salamishah Tillet, the first curated multi-artist public-art exhibition on the National Mall in Washington, D.C. (2023), and *Declaration House* in Philadelphia's Independence National Historical Park (2024) with Anna Arabindan-Kesson and Yolanda Wisher. Farber is the host and creator of *The Statue,* a podcast series from WHYY/NPR that was recognized as a Webby Honoree in Best Podcasts in the Arts & Culture. Farber is a senior research scholar at the Center for

Public Art and Space at the University of Pennsylvania Stuart Weitzman School of Design and holds a Ph.D. in American culture from the University of Michigan. He currently serves on the board of trustees of the Andrew W. Mellon Foundation (New York), board of directors of A Long Walk Home (Chicago), and advisory board of the Humboldt Forum (Berlin, Germany).

Poet, musician, educator, and curator **Yolanda Wisher** is the author of the poetry volume *Monk Eats an Afro* (2014). Wisher was named the inaugural Poet Laureate of Montgomery County, Pennsylvania, in 1999 and the third Poet Laureate of Philadelphia in 2016. A Pew and Cave Canem Fellow, Wisher received the Leeway Transformation Award in 2019 for her commitment to art for social change. In 2022, she was named a Philadelphia Cultural Treasures Artist Fellow. Wisher performs a blend of poetry and song with her band Yolanda Wisher & The Afroeaters. She works as senior curator at Monument Lab.

## CONTRIBUTORS

**Niya Bates** is a Ph.D. candidate in history and African American studies at Princeton University. She studies nineteenth- and twentieth-century U.S. history, global environmentalism, and rural cultural landscapes. Her dissertation seeks to connect Black landscapes in nineteenth-century Appalachia to global traditions of marronage. Prior to attending Princeton, Bates worked to preserve African American culture and historic sites in central Virginia and founded the Scuffletown Project. She also served as the director of the Getting Word African American History Department at Thomas Jefferson's Monticello. Bates was born and raised in central Virginia and descends from families who were enslaved in that area.

**Kerry C. Bickford** is a Philadelphia-based curator and artistic producer whose practice focuses on site-responsive public art and intersections between art and local ecology. She is currently an associate curator at the Brandywine Conservancy and Museum of Art. Prior to joining Brandywine, she served as a senior project manager at Monument Lab, where she produced *Declaration House* and the Monument Lab Summit. Bickford has also worked as the curator of Ecological Futures and the director of programs at Philadelphia Contemporary, where she curated or cocurated the projects *Jean Shin: Freshwater*; *Lenape Sippu: Call Her By Her Name*; *Tracey Emin: A Moment Without You*; *Commonwealth*; *Edward Burtynsky: Megaresources*; and *Ana Vizcarra Rankin: time/scale*. She has produced and coproduced numerous projects, including *Grounds that Shout! (and others merely shaking)* and *Jane Irish: Antipodes*. Bickford has an M.A. from the Williams Graduate Program in the History of Art and a B.A. in English and art history from Northwestern University.

**Paul Buchanan** is a queer, Afro-Caribbean writer with roots in Guyana and the American South. His primary interests lie in the intersections between Black identity formation and trauma and in navigating depictions of Black people within and without the Black literary tradition. Currently, he is extending his research surrounding Black family trauma narratives into a full paper and polishing a collection of poems. He has an M.F.A. from Temple University and a B.A. in Black studies and English from Swarthmore College, and he is a recipient of the John Russell Hayes Poetry Award and the Mellon Mays Undergraduate Fellowship.

**Sonya Clark** is the Winifred Arms Professor of Art at Amherst College in Massachusetts. Previously, she chaired the Craft/Material Studies Department at Virginia Commonwealth University for twelve years. A graduate of Amherst College, Cranbrook Academy of Art, and the School of the Art Institute of Chicago, she holds four honorary doctorates and has received awards from United States Artists, Pollock-Krasner Foundation, Trellis Foundation, Art Prize, and Anonymous Was a Woman, among others. She has been granted residencies and fellowships at the Smithsonian, Civitella Ranieri in Italy, Indigo Arts Alliance in Maine, Yaddo in New York, the American Academy in Rome, and Black Rock in Senegal, among others. Her work has been exhibited in more than five hundred museums and galleries worldwide.

**Andrew M. Davenport**, Ph.D., is the vice president for research and Saunders director of the Robert H. Smith International Center for Jefferson Studies at Thomas Jefferson's Monticello. He has published academic articles on Thomas Jefferson's death and legacies, Ralph Ellison in mid-century New York City, and the influences of Black literature on post–World War II culture. He has also published in *Lapham's Quarterly*, the *Los Angeles Review of Books*, and *Smithsonian Magazine*. Davenport serves on the board of directors of the American Agora Foundation (*Lapham's Quarterly*). He earned his doctorate in U.S. history from Georgetown University.

**Kai Davis** is a Black, Queer, multidisciplinary artist, educator, and the 2024–2025 Poet Laureate of Philadelphia. Her work explores Blackness, Queerness, womanhood, grief, and the many ways these themes converge. Davis has performed for TEDxPhilly, CNN, BET, PBS, and NPR, among others. She is a two-time international grand-slam champion, winning the Brave New Voices International Youth Poetry Slam in 2011 and the College Union Poetry Slam Invitational in 2016. In 2017, Davis received the Leeway Transformation Award for her years of work with art for social change in Philadelphia. She is currently a co-organizer and the creative director for The Philly Pigeon Late(ish) Poetry Show, which won the Poetry Foundation's Equity in Verse Grant in 2023. Her work has been published by 2 Pens & Lint (2012) and in *The Offing* (2018), *The Shade Journal* (2019), and *Mouths of Rain: An Anthology of Black Lesbian Thought* (2021), among others.

**Husnaa Haajarah Hashim** is a poet, interdisciplinary artist, educator, and student herbalist. Her work engages themes of transnationalism, matrilineality, and Black feminist theory through such mediums as handwork, collage, and prose. She enjoys facilitating creative writing workshops and curating accessible public arts programming. A Philadelphia Youth Poet Laureate (2017–2018), Hashim is the author of the chapbook *Honey Sequence* (2018). Her work has appeared in *Apiary Magazine*; the On Being Project; *Rookie Mag*; Elixr Coffee's *Heart on Your Sleeve* coffee sleeves; Short Édition's Short Story Dispenser vending machine in Paris, France; and elsewhere.

**J. Calvin Jefferson Sr.**, who is descended from the Grangers as well as the Hemingses of Monticello, grew up in Washington, D.C. After working for the U.S. Postal Service, he became an archivist for the National Archives and Records Administration, from which he retired in 2007 after thirty years. He did not learn of his family's connection to Monticello until 1996. He has a strong interest in his family history and continues research on the Hemings family, particularly Betty Brown and her descendants. He is currently a consultant for the Getting Word African American History Department at Monticello.

**Jabari Jefferson** is a mixed-media oil painter based in Washington, D.C. Jefferson's vibrant multimedia paintings and sculptures are layered with found mixed-media material, such as books, fabric, paper, ink, and acrylic and oil paints. His mixed-media process involves recycling, repurposing, and recontextualizing discarded items into contemporary art. Jefferson's works comprise painted figures, mixed-media surroundings, and such materials as previously owned clothes, children's books, paper collages, and other found objects collected throughout his travels. His process involves searching local communities for once-owned items and repurposing them into usable pieces that add to his overall palette of materials. Inspired by ritualistic practices, Jabari believes in the transfer of energy in the materials from their previous owners. His subject matter ranges from esoteric existences to racial politics and focuses on themes of self-engagement, self-education, exploration of Black culture and history, spirituality, and mythology. Much of his work exclusively features Black subjects together or alone. Spanning his different bodies of work, his subjects are surrounded by an array of shapes, recognizable objects, or landscapes that fluently move in and out of expressionism and abstraction. His recognizable maximalist approach allows him to discreetly place clues to his influences among the plethora of materials that compose his works.

**Gayle Jessup White** is the public relations and community engagement officer at Monticello, Thomas Jefferson's historic estate. A former award-winning television reporter and anchor, Jessup White started her career at *The New York Times*. She is the author of *Reclamation: Sally Hemings, Thomas Jefferson, and a Descendant's Search for Her Family's Lasting Legacy* (2021). She is a direct Jefferson descendant and is also related to two well-documented families enslaved at Monticello—the Hemingses and the Hubbards. A fourth-generation Washingtonian, she currently lives in Virginia.

**Jane Kamensky**, Ph.D., president and CEO of Thomas Jefferson's Monticello, is a leading historian of early America and the United States. For thirty years, she worked as a professor and higher-education leader, most recently as the Jonathan Trumbull Professor of American History at Harvard University. Kamensky is the author or editor of numerous books, including *A Revolution in Color: The World of John Singleton Copley* (2016), which won four major prizes and was a finalist for several others. Her most recent book, *Candida Royalle and the Sexual Revolution* (2024), was a finalist for the National Book Critics Circle Award for Biography.

**Matthew Jordan-Miller Kenyatta**, Ph.D., M.C.P.—or "Dr. Matt"—is the director and curator of Temple Contemporary at the Tyler School of Art and Architecture, where he teaches and curates work on placemaking, taste, and urban change. His forthcoming book *Black Urbanism: Palms Growing in Concrete* (University of Pennsylvania Press, 2027) explores how South Los Angeles emerged and remains a contemporary cultural mecca. His concepts of "Afrotechtonics" and "Blacklighting" appear in *The Black Geographic: Praxis, Resistance, Futurity* (2023), *Just Urban Design: The Struggle for a Public City* (2022), and *Journal of the American Planning Association*. He has served as a 21st Century Preservation Leaders Fellow with the U.S. Advisory Council on Historic Preservation and as a Philadelphia art commissioner.

**Salamishah Tillet** is a Distinguished Professor of Africana Studies & Creative Writing at Rutgers University, Newark, and a Pulitzer Prize–winning contributing critic-at-large at the *New York Times*. She is the former director of Express Newark, a center for art, design, and digital storytelling at Rutgers, and a cofounder of A Long Walk Home, an arts organization dedicated to empowering young people to end violence against girls and women. Tillet is the author of *Sites of Slavery: Citizenship and Racial Democracy in the Post–Civil Rights Imagination* (2012), *In Search of* The Color Purple*: The Story of an American Masterpiece* (2021), and the forthcoming *All the Rage: Nina Simone and the World She Made*.

**Auriana Woods** is a historian of nineteenth-century African American life and the director of the Getting Word African American History Department at Monticello, Thomas Jefferson's plantation home. While her work spans Black American history from slavery to freedom, she focuses on the domestic slave trade and its forced migration of enslaved people from the Upper South to the Lower South between 1800 and 1865, with a particular emphasis on the fugitive kinship practices that emerged in response to family separation. As a public-facing historian, she works to reconstruct traditional conceptions of American history and identity through filling historic silences with narratives of African American families, emphasizing their centrality in early American history and positioning chattel slavery as a founding national institution. Woods graduated from Columbia University with her M.A. in oral history and from Brown University with her B.A. in Africana studies.

# Index

Page references for illustrations are in *italics*.